"I'm so glad my good friend Chad Veach wrote *Worried about Everything Because I Pray about Nothing*. Packed full of personal stories and biblical truths, he not only teaches you how to pray, he also explains how prayer can help you navigate stress and uncertainty in every area of your life. Imagine how incredible your prayer life will be when you apply what you learn in this book—it will change your life forever!"

Robert Morris, senior pastor of Gateway Church and bestselling author
of *The Blessed Life, Beyond Blessed*, and *Take the Day Off*

"In his book *Worried about Everything Because I Pray about Nothing*, Chad Veach brings us back to a practice often overlooked and deemed unnecessary: prayer. He practically and powerfully reminds us that prayer grounds our faith, guides our steps, and guards are hearts as we navigate the earth in partnership with God."

Sadie Robertson Huff, author, speaker, and founder of Live Original

"Prayer unlocks God's peace, power, and purpose in our lives—so why is it so easy to let it fall to the wayside? This book shifts our focus from what's happening around us to what's going on inside of us. That is where true peace is found."

Steven Furtick, lead pastor of Elevation Church and *New York Times* bestselling author of *Crash the Chatterbox, Greater*, and *(Un)Qualified*

"Sometimes our most difficult situations can be solved with a simple biblical truth. Chad is right! Why worry and stress when prayer is all you need to overcome? This is a must-read for every follower of Christ."

Jentezen Franklin, senior pastor of Free Chapel
and *New York Times* bestselling author

"Chad is not only a close friend but also a mentor! The Spirit of Jesus runs through him daily, and God has been doing amazing work in His life! I pray you read this incredible book with an open mind and open heart to grow closer in your personal relationship with Jesus."

Russell Wilson, Seattle Seahawks Superbowl-winning quarterback

WORRIED ABOUT EVERYTHING BECAUSE I PRAY ABOUT NOTHING

HOW TO LIVE WITH PEACE AND PURPOSE INSTEAD OF STRESS AND BURNOUT

CHAD VEACH

BETHANYHOUSE

a division of Baker Publishing Group
Minneapolis, Minnesota

Published by Bethany House Publishers
11400 Hampshire Avenue South
Minneapolis, Minnesota 55438
www.bethanyhouse.com

Bethany House Publishers is a division of
Baker Publishing Group, Grand Rapids, Michigan

Printed in the United States of America

Library of Congress Cataloging-in-Publication Data
Names: Veach, Chad, author.
Title: Worried about everything because I pray about nothing : how to live with peace and
    purpose instead of stress and burnout / Chad Veach.
Description: Minneapolis, Minnesota : Bethany House Publishers, a division of Baker Publishing
    Group, [2022] | Includes bibliographical references.
Identifiers: LCCN 2022002388 | ISBN 9780764240188 (cloth) | ISBN 9780764240195
    (paperback) | ISBN 9781493437610 (ebook)
Subjects: LCSH: Prayer—Christianity.
Classification: LCC BV210.3 .V43 2022 | DDC 248.3/2—dc23/eng/20220215
LC record available at https://lccn.loc.gov/2022002388

Cover design by Roman Bozhko

The author is represented by Capital Literary.

Baker Publishing Group publications use paper produced from sustainable forestry practices and post-consumer waste whenever possible.

22   23   24   25   26   27   28   7   6   5   4   3   2   1

Julia,
without your love, belief, and prayers,
I really don't know where we'd be.

You are a rock. A constant source of encouragement
and support to me, our family, and our church.

There's no one like you. I love you.

Georgia, Winston, Maverick, and Clive,
I love listening to you pray.

And I love praying over each of you.
May God's will be done in your life.

Zoe,
I've always dreamed of building a church
that knows how to pray.

A house of prayer. Thank you for praying
with great fervor and faith.

Your prayers have helped people around the world.
Heaven will tell your story.

Contents

Contents

ONE

The one thing I forgot

This book, like a couple of my children, was not planned.

That might seem like an odd way to start a book (or a family), but the best things in life are often unexpected.

I thought I was going to write another book on leadership. That was the subject of my last one, and it's the focus of my podcast and newsletter. Prayer was not even on my radar. The *practice* of prayer was, of course, but not *writing* about it.

Why? Because prayer is one of those fundamental, indispensable things that we tend to take for granted. Like oxygen. Or water. Or Wi-Fi. (Okay, maybe Wi-Fi isn't on the same level as oxygen or water, but judging by my kids' reaction when the router goes down for fifteen minutes, you'd think it was.)

Something changed in mid-2020, though. I was in Alabama on a family vacation. We were staying in a house by a lake, and one morning, I was out on the deck, enjoying the sunrise, sipping my coffee, and reading my Bible.

And, of course, praying as I started the day.

After all, this is my morning routine, although I normally don't have a lake in front of me while I'm doing it. Usually, it's just the wall of my living room and maybe the face of a random child who woke up too early.

As I sat there and watched the colors change and the world wake up, God spoke to me. Nothing dramatic or audible, just a whispered thought in my heart. He told me to teach our people to pray.

That surprised me. What is there to teach?

Then I remembered a story in the Bible where Jesus went off to pray, which was a habit of His as well. I doubt He had coffee, but He was God, so He could stay awake without caffeine. He would be gone before His disciples woke up sometimes. Often nobody could find Him—neither the disciples nor the crowds—because He was wandering the hills or some nearby olive orchard, just praying.

On this occasion, when Jesus finished praying, His disciples were waiting for Him. There was something about His prayer life that captivated them. There was a massive difference between Jesus' private, authentic walk with God and the public, all-for-show prayers that often characterized the religious leaders of the day.

I think they wanted the same peace, passion, and power they saw in their Lord, and they realized that His prayer life was the catalyst for all of that. It was the secret sauce, the missing ingredient—and they wanted to know more.

When Jesus walked up to the group, one of them blurted out what they were all thinking: "Lord, teach us to pray" (Luke 11:1).

Frequently, when people asked Jesus a question or tried to get an easy rule to follow, He would reply with another question or with a parable. He wasn't being difficult, but rather requiring them to engage with the topic and explore it more in depth—not settle for superficial answers.

Jesus could have responded that way. He could have said, "Just do it. Learn as you go," or, "Study the Scriptures and figure it out for yourself."

But He didn't. He didn't roll His eyes or dodge their question. I think their hunger to pray thrilled His heart.

So Jesus taught them to pray. Think about that. Jesus, the perfect, divine teacher, put whatever plans He had on hold for that day just so He could teach His crew how to do what He did best: pray.

He gave them a simple, specific prayer. We call it the Lord's Prayer, but it was more than an empty formula to recite. It was a sample prayer. A template to follow. A starter pack for prayer newbies, if you will.

Why did Jesus take time to teach prayer? Because although prayer is vital to the Christian experience, it's easy to neglect, and it's not always intuitive.

On a basic level, prayer is not hard. Anyone can talk to God. That's why there are no atheists in foxholes, as the saying goes. But the nuances and intricacies of prayer take time to understand. We often have misconceptions that hinder our prayer. We have perspectives of God that are not healthy. We expect the wrong things from prayer or try to use it the wrong way.

When God spoke to me that morning by the lake, I started thinking back over my own prayer journey. I realized that I had specific moments when I *learned* to pray—sometimes on my own, and sometimes through the teaching and example of leaders in the faith.

I realized that prayer is a learned skill.

Prayer is a learned skill.

That's important because we can be intimidated by it sometimes. We can feel frustrated that we aren't better at it, or that we don't enjoy it more, or that we don't see more results. Nobody is born knowing how to pray, though. It takes practice and experience. You grow in it. You improve at it.

That really is the purpose for this book, to be honest: *to learn how to pray*. We will explore the purposes and practice of prayer and cover practical advice about how to pray.

As we begin, I'd like to share a few of those pivotal moments when God taught me to pray.

LUNCH AND PRAYER

My prayer journey starts when I was sixteen.

My parents were pastors in a small church in western Washington, so prayer, worship, preaching, Bible, church attendance, and other spiritual disciplines were familiar to me. I wasn't too interested, though. I didn't see the point of it all. I cared more about basketball, girls, SportsCenter, and the Seattle SuperSonics than I did about meeting with God in prayer.

And I was fine with that.

Ironically, during those teenage years, I couldn't shake the sense that I was going to be a pastor someday. I tried to ignore it. I told everyone I was going to be either a basketball coach or a DJ. Anything but a pastor. I was determined to pursue my own future, and I couldn't imagine church being a big part in that.

I was also deeply unhappy. I remember feeling lost, anxious, and unsettled. Even though I filled my life with friends and sports, I was unfulfilled. I wanted a change; I just didn't know what that looked like.

At age sixteen I attended a large Christian event called Promise Keepers, and I had a genuine encounter with God. Even now, nearly twenty-five years later, I don't know how to describe it other than to say that God made himself real to me, and nothing was ever the same.

Overnight, I found myself insatiably hungry for God. The stress and emptiness of my life drove me to prayer. Every night at ten o'clock, I would be on my knees next to my bed, praying to a God I was just beginning to know, with my Bible in front of me and worship music blasting in my ears from my Sony Walkman.

Yes, a Walkman. I'm that old. I had a Walkman back when they were cool, not "classic" or "vintage." Cassette tapes, Side A, Side B, fixing mangled and tangled tape with a pencil . . . if you know, you know.

Prayer was calming for me. It took me to a place of surrender. It settled my anxiety and filled the emptiness I had been feeling, giving me a love for God and others I had never felt before. I continued that nightly ritual for several months.

When I began my senior year of high school, I decided to organize a small prayer group during the lunch hour. It was a public high school with eighteen hundred students. I had no idea what I was doing, but I knew many kids who were struggling with pain, depression, and addictions, and I wanted them to find the same peace I had found. Praying for them seemed like the logical thing to do.

There were three of us at first: two friends and me. Lunch lasted thirty minutes, so every day, we'd eat for fifteen minutes, then go to an empty classroom and pray for fifteen minutes. When the bell rang, we'd head to class.

We weren't "good" at prayer. Our prayers were anything but eloquent. We were just three guys reaching out to God with the needs we saw in our friends, the school, and ourselves.

Soon, we invited a few more friends. Within a week there were five of us. Then seven. Then ten, twenty, thirty.

Word spread and people were curious, so more kids came to check it out. We had to move from the classroom to the choir room because we ran out of space. Even more students showed up: forty, then sixty, then eighty. We no longer fit in the choir room, so we moved to the gym.

The prayer time was open to anyone: freshmen, sophomores, juniors, and seniors. The jocks, the nerds, the goths, the stoners, the misfits, the new kids, the popular kids. People who were lonely. People who knew they weren't doing well. People looking for acceptance, comfort, or strength.

All were welcome, and all came.

We didn't preach or share anything from the Bible, we just offered to pray for needs. Kids would ask for prayer for a sick relative, a big test, a drug addiction, a breakup, a big football game. Then me or a buddy would pray for the requests.

And God showed up.

Young people were set free from anorexia and alcoholism. Dozens of kids were saved. We met God in a real, transforming way. I can think of six or seven pastors in ministry today who were present in those lunchtime prayer meetings. That year of simple, unscripted prayer times marked us forever.

WANDERING THE MOUNTAINS OF LA

My second major experience with prayer began right after I graduated from high school. By this time, I had accepted the call of God on my life to ministry. I loved basketball (and still do today), but I realized I wasn't called to teach kids how to shoot or dribble. I was called to pastor people.

I was invited by a church in East Los Angeles to come work with their youth ministry. I ended up being there for six years, and I enjoyed every minute of it. I fell in love with the people; they didn't have a lot of money, but they were hardworking, courageous, and full of life.

During this period, I met an Argentinian man named Yoel Bartolomé. We worked together at a church in California, and he became a close mentor. Every couple of weeks, we would meet at a gas station at six in the morning, then drive up to the San Gabriel Mountains. We would split up and wander the mountainside, praying and seeking God.

Like the lunchroom prayer times, those mountaintop moments became part of the fabric of my walk with God. Being outdoors and surrounded by creation is always a good reminder that there is someone bigger than you out there. Maybe that's what Jesus was doing when He would sneak away to the mountains to pray: He was connecting with a God whose power, like His love, is limitless.

In high school, I met a personal God. He knew my name and cared about my needs.

In the mountains, I met a big God. A sovereign, missional God who didn't just know my name and care for me, but who loved the world. A God who wanted to use my life as part of His plan.

PRAYING FOR PUYALLUP

The mountaintop prayer times were a highlight of my season in East LA. But that stage of life came to an end when, in 2004, I moved to Puyallup, Washington, a town of thirty-five thousand people south of Seattle, known for hosting the Washington State Fair and having the world's greatest scones. Seriously. I miss those scones.

I had been offered a job at a church in Puyallup. I knew it was the right decision, but to be honest, I didn't want to go. Nothing against Puyallup, but I was in love with LA. The way the city moved, the people, the culture, the weather, the palm trees, the Lakers, the food. Seemed like a lot to trade for scones.

I remember leaving LA, driving north on the freeway, and complaining to God about where life was taking me. Suddenly, He interrupted my rant. I can't really put the experience into words; I just knew it was Him.

He spoke to me specifically: _"You'll move back here one day. You'll start a church, and you'll live here for the rest of your life."_

Just then, my cell phone rang. It was Mom. She said, "Chad, I was praying for you right now, and God spoke to me. He said you're going to move back to LA someday, start a church, and live the rest of your life there."

Tears began to flow. I could hardly see to drive. The sense of loss was replaced by an assurance of sovereign calling. The anxiety and frustration had given way to peace. I knew in that instant that every season was in His hands, every step planned out by Him. God was going to lead me and use me in Puyallup.

I began working with the young people in the church. We met Sunday nights because the weeknights were too full of school activities.

My Sunday routine was to go to church in the morning, head home to change, play basketball for a couple of hours, then go straight to church at three o'clock to set up for the youth service, which started at seven. I would put on worship music and set up the chairs while I prayed over each one.

Soon I invited a couple of young people to join me for prayer. For forty-five minutes, we would walk around the room and pray for the service. Sometimes we would sit or lie on the floor, seeking God and praying for our generation. Eventually more people started coming to pray, until fifteen or twenty of us were meeting together every Sunday afternoon at three o'clock.

We did that for nine years. Again, God showed up.

There were twenty-four students at our first Sunday night youth meeting. Within nine months, there were six hundred. During those nine years, thousands of young people met Jesus, built relationships, and found peace. Their lives were changed, and the effects of those changes rippled out into their families and friends. Eventually we hosted an annual youth conference, produced our own music, and much more.

It was beyond anything I dreamed of when I left LA. It was astronomically greater than I could have imagined as a senior in high school, leading prayer meetings during lunch. This was completely supernatural. There's no other way to explain it.

GEORGIA

Puyallup ended up being a beautiful, sovereign season of my life. Not just because of the church, though. There I met and married my wife, Julia, in

2008. Julia is my partner in everything. She's my rock, my inspiration, my hero. She's the greatest thing that has ever happened to me outside of Jesus.

In 2011, our daughter, Georgia, was born. Four months later, she was diagnosed with lissencephaly, or smooth brain, a rare disorder that affected her brain development. I wrote about Georgia and our journey with her health challenges in my book _Unreasonable Hope_.

Talk about a sledgehammer to the heart! That news—and the months after—were challenging, to say the least. Prayer took on new meaning for me through this experience. You'd think that I would have been angry with God or desperate for a solution, and that my prayers would have reflected that. There were certainly moments where that was the case. But overall, there was a deep sense of the presence and grace of God in our lives.

When I prayed for Georgia, I would sense God's assurance not that she would be healed, but that she wasn't broken. She was perfect, beautiful, and loved.

I learned in that season that prayer is about much more than just getting answers or miracles from God. It's about _being_ with Him, about receiving peace and strength and life directly from Him.

In 2014, after a brief season in Seattle getting our feet on the ground and preparing for the future, we moved to LA to start a church. The promise I had heard from God when I was praying (or more accurately, complaining, although complaining is also a valid form of prayer!) as I drove toward Puyallup years earlier was finally coming true.

Zoe Church (pronounced zō-AY) launched in 2015, and it has been a wild, beautiful, awesome ride. Julia and I know we are called to serve people and to raise up a healthy, community-loving church. We are not the experts on faith or church. We have not "arrived" at some place of success. (Does anyone? Ever?) Instead, we are constantly learning from and growing with the people around us.

One of those learning moments happened in 2019 when I visited an incredible church in Bogotá, Colombia, pastored by Andrés Corson, which over forty thousand people attended. The presence of God was tangible in their meetings. I heard story after story of people who had been changed by the power of God. It was beyond inspiring, not just because of the size, but because of the influence and the move of God that was so evident.

Their church is named *El Lugar de Su Presencia*, or The Place of His Presence. I love that. It's a reflection of their commitment, not to religion, an organization, or a pastor, but to *God himself*. To His presence, His will, His love.

One of the things that most stood out to me, though, was their early morning prayer meeting. I've been to quite a few morning prayer times in my life. Usually there are a handful of half-awake, zombie-like, faithful people in a room, some of them seeking God and the others dreaming about a hot breakfast. Or both, if we're honest.

That wasn't the case in Bogotá, though. They told me that about *three thousand* people met to pray every Tuesday and Thursday at 6:00 a.m., all year round, year after year. No wonder the church was experiencing God's presence in such a real way. No wonder it was having an impact on the city and nation around it.

THE MISSING PIECE

That morning by the lake, while the day grew hotter and my coffee got colder, I remembered every one of those moments. The lunchtime prayer groups. The mountains outside East LA. The 3:00 p.m. prayer sessions in Puyallup. The long nights praying for Georgia. The church in Bogotá.

Then, I felt like God asked me, "What makes a great person? What makes a great church?"

Things like love, faith, character, generosity, and wisdom came to mind. But as God took me back over those life-altering experiences with Him, I realized I was missing something.

I was missing prayer.

Prayer had been at the heart of every encounter with God and every season of ministry. It was the overlooked element that grounded my faith, guided my steps, and guarded my heart. It was the reason kids spent half their lunchtime in a gym. It was the reason our youth group exploded from twenty-four people to over six hundred. It was the power behind the church in Bogotá and other churches around the world.

I heard God say simply, "Chad, this year, add prayer to the church."

Our church has great people, great leaders, great ministries. We were doing many good things for people in our community. Now, though, it was time to grow in prayer. Both as a church and as individuals, God was asking us to meet Him and to know Him better through prayer.

The next week, I taught our staff meeting on the topic of prayer. A couple months later, I started a sermon series about prayer. We also created a prayer card to hand out to our church (it's included in the back of this book). We ramped up our regular, focused prayer times like never before.

Now I'm writing a book about prayer. Unexpectedly, yes—but enthusiastically.

My focus in these pages will be how prayer can help you navigate the stress, uncertainty, and blind curves in all areas of life. We will look at how prayer involves God in every facet of our day-to-day existence, including our emotions, finances, faith, ministry, and more.

I'm a pastor, but first, I'm a husband and father and neighbor and friend and boss and Lakers fan and overall normal human being. I've found that prayer has a place in all the spheres of my life. Especially the Lakers sphere. (Come on, if you don't pray for your team, are you even a real fan?)

The same goes for you.

Regardless of your age, gender, financial picture, marital status, career aspirations, favorite sports team, or any other variable, you need prayer. You will come to love prayer (if you don't already!). Prayer connects you to God, and being connected to Him changes everything.

As you read, keep in mind that terms like *anxiety* and *fear* are used across a wide spectrum of behavior, emotion, and mental health. The last thing I want to do is imply that I have easy answers for problems that are beyond my knowledge or training.

I'm also not saying that prayer should replace other tangible actions and strategies. That kind of superficial, cheap dismissal is called spiritual bypassing, and it does a huge disservice to prayer. I have an entire chapter on that later on.

Prayer does not undermine the importance of therapy, medicine, or other treatment. Quite the opposite. I have deep respect for therapists, psychologists, doctors, scientists, and other experts in their respective fields who are contributing to our understanding of these complex emotions.

Prayer connects you to God, and being connected to Him changes everything.

I believe that healing, like truth, is multifaceted. That is, God often brings restoration through multiple sources of growth and understanding at the same time. Prayer and science are not mutually exclusive. They work together.

Don't stop doing whatever is working for you. Keep learning and growing. Find and use whatever tools you can to navigate what you're facing.

But in that search, don't overlook prayer! You can always add more prayer to your life, and you might be surprised how much it helps.

Prayer was never meant to be associated with stuffy church services or fancy religious language. It has always been a way for *real* people to talk with a *real* God about *real* issues.

No matter who you are or what you're facing, I believe growing in your prayer life will change you, just as it has changed me and so many others. Not because prayer is some magical activity in and of itself, but because prayer connects you to God.

Prayer is the vehicle, not the destination. It's the method, not the goal.

God himself is the destination and the goal. Prayer just gets you closer to Him.

The goal of this book, then, is to simplify prayer, not to complicate it. It's to place it back where it belongs, which is wherever you and I are at. Prayer was meant for _us_, after all. It's our God-given privilege, our gift, and our responsibility.

I truly believe you are already a great person in God's eyes. You have come far, you have done much, you have lived in faith and love. God wants to increase who you are, not change it. He wants to expand your heart and your capacity and your calling. He wants to add prayer to the incredible person you've become.

You're going to love where prayer takes you—no matter how unplanned or unexpected that might be.

PRAYER CHANGES EVERYTHING . . . BUT MAINLY YOU

When I was a teenager, my parents existed mainly to provide things for me.

I'm sure that when my kids hit their teen years, I'm going to be on the receiving end of that mentality. As a teenager, you don't think about your parents too often unless you need something from them, or when they are getting in the way of you doing what you want. It's the law of adolescence.

Luckily, that changes. You grow up. You get a job. You develop empathy and a smidge of humility. You have kids of your own and suddenly wish you would have given your parents more grace.

You discover that *who they are* to you matters far more than *what they give you*. I'm a grown man with a family, house, and job of my own. I don't "need" my parents to give me anything. But my relationship with them is genuine, deep, fulfilling, and vital. The way I value them has changed dramatically since I was a teenager.

Mark Twain is often quoted as saying, "When I was a boy of fourteen, my father was so ignorant I could hardly stand to have the old man around. But when I got to be twenty-one, I was astonished at how much the old man had learned in seven years."

If I'm honest, sometimes I've viewed God the way I viewed my parents.

At first, He was there to provide for my needs, but that was about it.

But I've changed. I've grown up, so to speak. And now I'm astonished at how much God means to me, how much He does, and how important my relationship with Him has become. I've learned that, like my parents, *who God is* matters far more than *what He gives me*.

So if I pray just to get something from God, I'm missing out on most of what prayer is for.

In the following chapters, we're going to explore the benefits of prayer. We'll ask questions like, "Why do I need God?" and "What is prayer good for?"

You'll notice that the last chapter is the only one that talks about *answered* prayer. Answered prayer is awesome, of course. But it's actually far down the list of importance. The rest of the chapters focus on what prayer does *in, through,* and *for* us. In the grand scheme of your life, those are the things that matter most.

Prayer changes things.

Mostly you.

TWO

Relaxing on a roller coaster

Prayer and peace

I can still remember playing hide-and-seek with my friends as a kid. I would hide under a bed or in a closet while someone counted to ten. Then the person would stalk the house in search of a victim.

After a few moments, I would inevitably hear footsteps right beside the bed or outside the closet. It would strike me—too late—that, like a total newbie, I had chosen the most obvious hiding place in the room.

I would be as terrified as if I were hiding from an actual ax murderer. My heart would dislodge itself from its normal spot inside my chest and make its way up my throat. There would be nothing to do but hold my breath and hope the "seeker" assumed no one would be stupid enough to hide where I was.

Naturally, that would be the moment I had an irresistible urge to cough.

Two minutes later, I would find myself counting to ten while my friends ran and hid. But at least now it was my turn to inflict terror on the rest of the group.

Isn't it odd that our idea of a good time as kids was to intentionally put ourselves into terrifying situations? This fixation with fear doesn't stop when we grow up, though. As adults, we'll pay a therapist a hundred dollars to help us work through our anxiety—and the next day, we'll pay a theme park another hundred dollars to scare the crud out of us on a roller coaster. And somehow that makes perfect sense.

If our twisted idea of fun teaches us anything, it's that fear is a normal part of the human experience. We were actually built to handle a certain level of fear, anxiety, stress, and worry. God gave us the capacity to navigate the uncertainties of life without losing our mind.

The presence of fear is not the problem. The problem is when our fear gets so overwhelming that it snuffs out our *peace*.

Unfortunately, that happens far too often. I think it's safe to say that most of us have too much worry and too little peace in our day-to-day existence.

As I write this, we are a year and a half into a global pandemic that seems to be getting worse, not better. At the same time, racial disparity, political disagreements, international conflicts, world disasters, climate change, and other complex and urgent issues are filling our minds as well. The constant stimulation from our social media feeds only adds to the mental and emotional barrage.

Is it just me, or does all of this feel overwhelming? We are worried about everything—because everything is worrisome.

In 2020, the American Psychological Association released their annual "Stress in America" report. Before launching into a ten-page description of the rise in anxiety and stress that the United States is facing (and the rest of the world, we could add), the article lists the stressors that are weighing on people's minds and then states bluntly, "It is the unusual combination of these factors and the persistent drumbeat of a crisis that shows no sign of abating that is leading APA to sound the alarm: We are facing a national mental health crisis that could yield serious health and social consequences for years to come."[1]

Their numbers only prove what most of us probably already sense: There is a crazy amount of stress in our lives. There are far too many reasons to worry.

So how do we navigate a world that is so uncertain? How do we process the normal fears and stressors of life in a healthy way? How do we remain confident that things are going to turn out okay, that we will come out on the other side, that we are enough for the task? How do we relax on this roller coaster called life?

We don't need to eliminate fear. We just need something _bigger_ than fear.

We need true peace.

GOD OF PEACE

Sure, you might be thinking. _That's easy for you to say. Peace would be great. But how do I find a peace that is bigger than the things I'm going through?_

Well, I'd like to suggest an under-recognized but highly effective source of peace: prayer.

I'm sure you saw that coming, since the title of this book is literally _Worried about Everything Because I Pray about Nothing._ But hear me out.

Prayer is truly one of the best ways to find peace, and peace is one of the most immediate, visible results of prayer. If you need peace, _pray._

You might need to do more than pray, but definitely don't do less.

You might need to do more than pray, but definitely don't do less.

I promise you that prayer will make a difference. I can't begin to count the number of times I've gone from panic to peace in a matter of minutes, simply by praying through my fears.

Jesus told the crowds who listened to Him, "Come to me, all you who are weary and burdened, and I will give you rest. Take my yoke upon you and learn from me, for I am gentle and humble in heart, and you will find rest for your souls" (Matthew 11:28–29).

The practice of prayer doesn't produce fleeting, superficial peace; it produces true peace. Lasting peace. Soul-level peace. When we come to God, we find peace for our inner self. We find peace for the soul. Our circumstances might not change, but our souls find peace.

On another occasion, Jesus told His disciples, "Peace I leave with you; my peace I give you. I do not give to you as the world gives. Do not let your hearts be troubled and do not be afraid" (John 14:27).

Jesus knew they were anxious about the future, and He wanted to remind them that the antidote to that anxiety was not external change, but an internal connection with God. That divine peace is greater than any source or form of peace the world has to offer.

In both of these passages, Jesus portrays himself as the source of peace.

That's important because prayer is our real-time link to God. Things like mindfulness, journaling, and yoga often focus on connecting you with yourself and the world around you, which is important. But prayer connects you to *God*.

That's an entirely different level of wholeness and peace.

Prayer is not empty words whispered into the wind. It's not a relaxation technique. Prayer is such a powerful channel of peace because it brings us into the presence of a real, present, caring, active, sovereign God.

When we pray, we are interacting with the God of peace. That title—"God of peace"—appears several times in the Bible, and it's one of my favorites.

"The God of peace be with you all. Amen" (Romans 15:33).

"The God of peace will soon crush Satan under your feet" (Romans 16:20).

"The God of peace will be with you" (Philippians 4:9).

"May God himself, the God of peace, sanctify you through and through" (1 Thessalonians 5:23).

In this crazy world, we long for peace on all levels. We want internal peace and external peace. We want financial peace, physical peace, emotional peace, spiritual peace, family peace, and world peace.

We won't fully find that peace, though, if we are seeking it in our own strength. The world is simply too big, too far outside our control.

That's where prayer really shines.

Prayer leads us to a God whose ways are higher than ours and whose power is greater than ours. It doesn't bypass our abilities, resources, strength, or wisdom, but it does go beyond them. Prayer reminds us that we don't have to rely on ourselves to make it through the messiness of life.

We are not alone. We are never alone.

PEACE > ANSWERS

The passage that inspired this book is Philippians 4:6–7:

> **Don't worry about anything; instead, pray about everything.** Tell God what you need, and thank him for all he has done. Then you will experience God's peace, which exceeds anything we can understand. His peace will guard your hearts and minds as you live in Christ Jesus. (NLT, emphasis added)

Notice the direct connection between taking our worries to God in prayer and receiving His peace, which is a peace that "exceeds anything we can understand," a peace that "will guard [our] hearts and minds." Paul says that when you feel anxious, that's a sign you need to pray. And when you pray, you receive peace.

I often go to prayer thinking I need results—but I come away from prayer with peace.

And that is far better.

Why? Because answered prayer only produces temporary peace and momentary relief. It's wonderful when it happens, but if we're honest with ourselves, we know that more problems are around the corner.

The peace of God, however, supersedes my circumstances. It assures me that even if my immediate situation hasn't changed, God is bigger than that situation, and He is worthy of my trust. Maybe I'll get the answer I want from my prayer, maybe I won't. But I have peace. And that peace is enough.

I still pray for what I need and want, of course, but I don't try to get my peace from answered prayer. I get my peace from *God*.

Pray yourself to peace. He is the source of the answers. He is the focus of my hope. He is the only one big enough to truly take care of me and my loved ones. No matter how bizarre or nerve-wracking life gets, God doesn't change. And since I know Him, I know peace.

If you've looked at prayer as mostly about begging God for what you want or need, it's time to change your focus.

Don't just seek answers. Seek peace.

And don't just seek any peace. Seek the peace that exceeds understanding, the peace that comes from the God of peace himself.

So yes, go on roller coasters, if that's your thing. And if you have kids, play hide-and-seek with them and teach them the fine art of scaring each other half to death.

But don't lose your peace.

Don't let the cares and worries of an uncertain world overwhelm the calm assurance that God is with you.

You have a Father in heaven who knows you, cares about you, and watches over you. He alone can bring rest to your soul, and that rest is always available through prayer.

Don't worry yourself to death.

Pray yourself to peace.

Pour your own cereal

Prayer and purpose

I have a lot of kids. Four, last time I counted, but it feels like more than that. They currently range in age from three to ten, so as you can imagine, they keep my wife, Julia, and me busy.

One thing I've noticed about kids is that they have elevated complaining to an art form. Adults complain too, of course, but kids are less subtle about it.

It's good that they are insistent and loud, though. Otherwise they might never be heard. After all, their mouths are only three feet off the ground, so shouting toward the sky is the key to getting the adults around them to grant their requests. From a very young age—as in, from the moment they draw their first breath—they learn how to use their lungs, and eventually their words, to get what they want.

Some people treat prayer like that. They seem to think that if they shout up at the sky, if they whine and wail loudly enough and long enough, God will finally pay attention to them and grant their requests.

There are two problems with that mentality. First, unlike human parents, God has an unlimited capacity to pay attention to us and care for us. He is the ultimate multitasker. He doesn't get tired like we do. He doesn't lose His temper like we do. He doesn't think back longingly to days when He didn't have kids, when He could sleep in late, watch movies that were (gasp) not animated, and go out without finding a babysitter. . . .

But I digress. Parenting is awesome. I remind myself of that often.

My point is that we don't have to whine and complain and pester God until He finally does what we want. He's already on our side. He knows and cares about our needs before we even think to pray about them.

The second problem is that complaining can be a way of escaping personal responsibility. As my kids have gotten older, I've found myself doing something that I'm sure my parents used to do.

I hand their requests back to them.

"You're hungry? Wow, we literally ate dinner fourteen minutes ago. But I get it, you're growing. Well, you know how to make a bowl of cereal. Go for it. Let me know if you need help reaching the milk."

"You can't find your lunchbox? Weird. That has only happened ninety-four times this school year. Did you look in your backpack? Under your bed? In the closet? Go look again. If you still can't find it, go ask Mom to help. Just kidding. I'll help you. But also ask Mom. Just don't tell her I sent you."

"You're bored? I'm sorry, bud. But you know, this isn't a Disney vacation, and I'm not your entertainment director. You've got a room full of toys. Get creative. When I was a kid, electricity hadn't even been invented yet, and we still had fun."

I'm exaggerating for the sake of emphasis, of course. I'm a lot nicer and less sarcastic than that. (That might change when they are teenagers because snark and sarcasm are teenagers' love languages, so check back with me in a few years.) But I do encourage and expect my kids, in an age-appropriate way, to do what I know they are capable of doing.

Refusing to do for my kids what they can do for themselves is not bad parenting. It's *good* parenting. As parents, we train our kids to take responsibility for themselves. They might groan now, but someday they'll thank us for it. Well, maybe they'll never verbally thank us, but two or three decades down the road, they'll do the same thing for their kids.

I love seeing my children grow up and become more independent. It's normal. It's healthy. It's exciting. I want them to believe in themselves. I enjoy challenging them to do more, and I delight in watching them succeed. They enjoy it too, once they learn a new skill or gain new freedom.

I don't ask them to do more than they are capable of. But I might ask them to do more than they *think* they can do or more than they *want* to do. They need that. Our role as parents is not to do everything for our kids, but to help them believe in their own abilities and to encourage them in their purpose.

In an interview with inc.com, Dr. Stephanie O'Leary, a clinical psychologist and author of *Parenting in the Real World: The Rules Have Changed*, insisted that letting children struggle, even fail, benefits them far more than doing everything for them. She stated, "Your willingness to see your child struggle communicates that you believe they are capable and that they can handle any outcome, even a negative one."[1]

Our kids need to know that they are more than able to be successful on their own. They need supportive parents, yes, but they don't need helicopter parents hovering overhead, making sure they are constantly happy and always perfect.

They might be frustrated in the moment, but the very fact that you believe in them enough to let them muddle through is teaching them self-confidence. Plus, by trying and failing and trying again, they learn problem-solving, perseverance, and a bit of humility.

Those are invaluable gifts. Now, if we as parents realize that, don't you think God does too?

In case you haven't noticed, God is not a helicopter God. He's always there, of course, but He's not anxiously controlling our progress, stepping in to fix our mistakes when we color outside the lines, or yelling at us when we accidentally shatter a flower vase.

God continually encourages us to try new things, to fail, to learn, to try again, to grow. He's with us and for us, but He doesn't do everything for us. Instead, He cheers us on as we move forward in our purpose.

PRAYER AND PURPOSE

Purpose. Think about that word for a moment. It implies a potential, a calling, a goal. It means participating in life, not just letting life happen.

Good parents don't just protect and provide for their kids. They help them find and achieve purpose. That includes purpose in the general sense of becoming a responsible human, but also purpose in a more specific sense, by inspiring them to dream big and nudging them to pursue their dreams.

When it comes to prayer, doesn't it make sense that our heavenly Father would also hand many of our requests back to us? That He would look beyond our immediate comfort and instead point us toward our purpose? That He would tactfully ignore the whining and remind us that we are capable, creative, well-resourced people made in His image?

In other words, God doesn't do everything for us, but He works with us to do everything that needs to be done. It's a partnership.

When we pray about what is worrying us, God usually involves us in the solution of the very thing we are praying for. Don't be surprised if your prayer times morph into brainstorming sessions. That might be God gently nudging you into action.

If prayer rarely leads to action, you're doing it wrong.

Some of my most creative moments have come from prayer. They didn't start in creativity, of course. They started with whining. With me telling God how much a particular situation sucked and how He clearly needed to intervene.

But they ended with me pacing the room, excitedly dreaming about how we could solve a problem that fifteen minutes earlier seemed overwhelming.

If peace is the first benefit we receive from prayer, as we saw in the last chapter, purpose is a close second. The two go hand in hand.

Peace refers to the assurance that God has a plan. *Purpose* refers to the part you and I play in that plan.

Both are beautiful.

God is committed to awakening our purpose and prodding us toward it. He knows what we can do, even if we don't think we can do it. God cares about our present *and* our future. He sees the purpose, the plans, the potential written all over our lives. He placed those things within us, after all, and He calls them into existence day by day.

When you go to God in prayer, you walk away with purpose. He gives you direction, guidance, instructions, challenges. He shows you dreams to chase and giants to conquer.

Don't ask God to guide your steps if you're not ready to get off the couch.

LET'S DO IT TOGETHER

This principle that God involves us in the answers to our own prayers helps resolve a common misconception about prayer: that we either ask God to do something or we do it ourselves, but not both.

Usually, when we face a problem, we try to solve it ourselves. When that doesn't work, we call out to God in prayer for help. But if He doesn't answer right away, we get frustrated and decide we're going to handle it on our own. And so on and so forth, swinging like a pendulum between the "God will do it" and "I will do it" extremes.

But those two options—God does it or I do it—are a false dichotomy. That is, they are not the only two options. They are also not mutually exclusive.

When it comes to fixing problems, does God do it, or do I do it?

Yes.

It's almost always both/and. We work and pray, and pray and work, and work and pray because _life is a partnership with God._ The beauty and mystery of prayer are found in that partnership

We can't separate God's work from ours, which is why we can't separate prayer from action.

of purpose. We can't separate God's work from ours, which is why we can't separate prayer from action.

> _We_ pray according to _His_ will. (1 John 5:14)
>
> _We_ ask for _His_ heavenly purposes to come to pass on the earth. (Luke 11:2)
>
> _We_ know and follow _His_ voice. (John 10:27)
>
> _He_ created good works beforehand for _us_ to walk in them. (Ephesians 2:10)
>
> _He_ has called _us_ according to _His_ purpose. (Romans 8:28)

Can you see how connected all of this is? What _we_ do and what _God_ does are literally inseparable.

God doesn't compartmentalize responsibilities the way we do. We like to divvy up the to-do list: "Okay, God, you're going to take care of this, and I'm going to take care of that. . . ."

And God just interrupts with a laugh. "No, let's do all of those things together. It's more fun that way."

Have you ever wondered, _Why should I even pray if God already knows every-thing? He has the perfect plan anyway. If I pray for something outside that plan, won't I just mess things up?_

The answer lies in this concept of purpose and partnership with God. We pray because that connection point involves us in the purpose God has for us. It gets us in on the ground floor, before anything has even happened yet. Prayer helps us understand His will, believe His will, and be empowered to do His will. Then we go out and actually do His will. As I said, God's role and our roles are inseparable.

Our prayers, like our actions, should be in alignment with His will. It's something we do together. Neither our prayers nor our actions should be disconnected from God. Rather, from the moment we pray until the moment we act, we are in this thing together with God.

YOU'LL KNOW IN YOUR KNOWER

The purpose that prayer gives us usually falls into one of two broad categories: long-term direction or short-term instructions.

Long-term direction is the idea of vision and calling. At times God will drop into your heart a sense of His purpose for this season or a coming season of life. I can't really tell you what that feels like because it's different every time and for everyone. You just "know in your knower," as my dad used to say.

What are the long-term areas where God might reveal purpose? Usually these are areas that have a significant impact on you or those around you, which means you want to get them right. That means praying about them *and* getting confirmation from other sources as well. (We'll talk about how to hear the voice of God in a later chapter.)

Some areas where you might want to seek long-term direction include:

1. Education and career
   This includes both the initial direction for your occupation as well as significant career changes later on. God cares about your work. He doesn't divide things up into secular vs. sacred like we tend to do. Take time to pray about your employment or business and listen for God's voice. He wants to guide you.

2. Calling and ministry

God gives each of us spiritual gifts that are meant to be used for the benefit of others (see 1 Corinthians 12 and Romans 12:3–8). Prayer is one of the primary ways of discovering those gifts.

3. Marriage and family

Having a spouse or kids doesn't change your value before God, of course, but it certainly qualifies as a big decision. If you want to get married or are already married, pray for your spouse. If you want kids or have kids, pray nonstop for them too. (By the way, if you don't have kids but you do have a dog you are convinced is "just like a child," then yes, pray for your pet. But I've had dogs and kids, and believe me, they are not the same.)

Long-term direction tends to be general. It's more of a big-picture idea of where God is leading you sometime in the future. _Short-term instructions_, on the other hand, are specific, immediate steps you should take in a particular area or decision.

When you spend time in prayer, you will gain understanding about what your next step needs to be. Again, I can't tell you exactly how you'll know. It's something you learn over time. Prayer opens up your mind and heart to God's wisdom, and it will often be a catalyst to determine tangible, actionable steps.

Usually, you'll see just the next step or two, though. God won't lay out your entire future in a detailed, fully illustrated handbook. If He did, you'd probably laugh in His face or quit on the spot.

He will give you purpose, then partner with you to fulfill that purpose.

Instead, God will lead you and accompany you along the way. King David, who had a lot of experience in knowing and following God's voice, wrote this in Psalm 32:8–9:

> I will instruct you and teach you in the way you should go;
> I will counsel you with my loving eye on you.

> Do not be like the horse or the mule,
>> which have no understanding
> but must be controlled by bit and bridle
>> or they will not come to you.

In other words, God wants to guide you. He wants to instruct, teach, and counsel you, to use the terms in this passage. And He does it all from a place of love.

God will lead you if you take the time to listen. He will give you purpose, then partner with you to fulfill that purpose.

Pray. Work. Repeat. You and God together are unstoppable.

God is not your dentist

Prayer and premise

There are certain occupations that I appreciate and hate at the same time. At the top of the list: dentists.

There is nothing remotely enjoyable, relaxing, or pleasant about someone cranking open your mouth so they can poke you with sharp metal objects and power tools. Going to the dentist is misery from the moment that blue vinyl chair tilts backward to the final swish-and-spit. To add insult to injury, you have to pay them. Your mouth feels like it's made of Styrofoam, and you can't talk without severing your tongue, but you still have to shell out money that would otherwise put your kid through college.

If you're a dentist, this isn't personal. I'm glad you exist. You're a gift to humanity. Keep up the good work. If we meet and I don't smile at you, though, it's not you. It's just that your occupation triggers the whole fight-or-flight thing in my brain.

I'm also subconsciously afraid you're judging my dental hygiene. You see, one of the main reasons I dislike going to the dentist (other than the aforementioned sharp objects and drills) is the shame that always seems to be associated with the experience.

Maybe it's my imagination, maybe it's my guilty conscience about not brushing enough, maybe I was traumatized as a kid—I don't know. All I know is that I never walk away from a visit to the dentist feeling encouraged about my brushing or flossing habits. Quite the opposite. I feel like a failure, like I'll never measure up to the holy standards of the American Dental Association.

Therefore, I avoid visiting the dentist. Why would I go somewhere that makes me feel bad about myself?

Many people treat God the same way. They feel shame when they think of Him, so they avoid Him. They think He's always judging their soul hygiene.

That's not exactly healthy for their prayer lives, of course.

FROM VS. FOR

Our beliefs about God—about His character, His attitude toward us, His value system, His desires—shape the premises for our prayers.

In other words, the way we see God determines the way we approach Him.

Read that again: The way we see God determines the way we approach God.

Similarly, our beliefs about ourselves—our worth, our standing, our potential, our importance—also shape our premises for prayer. The way we see ourselves will influence what we ask for and how we ask it.

These two things—our view of God and our view of ourselves—are pretty much inseparable. We rarely put words to them, but they lie at the base of how we pray, what we ask for, how much faith we have that God hears us, and whether we obey God when He speaks.

If we think we are failures, and we believe that God is mostly concerned about failure, we will avoid Him. We won't talk to Him. Why would we? That would be like making friends with the dentist. (I'm kidding. Dentists are people too.)

The way we see God determines the way we approach Him.

Even if we do pray, we'll probably spend most of our time and energy trying to convince God to forgive us, to like us, and to bless us.

That's not how Jesus prayed. It's not how Paul or other Bible characters prayed either. For example, listen to this prayer of Paul's for the Ephesian believers:

> And I pray that you, being rooted and established in love, may have power, together with all the Lord's holy people, to grasp how wide and long and high and deep is the love of Christ, and to know this love that surpasses knowledge—that you may be filled to the measure of all the fullness of God.
>
> Ephesians 3:17–19

Can you hear the boldness, confidence, and joy in his tone? He wasn't apologetic. He didn't grovel. He was convinced of God's love and power toward His people, and he was passionate about convincing others of it too.

Here's what I've noticed. Paul, Jesus, and many other heroes of the faith prayed *from*, not *for*.

From God's forgiveness, not *for* His forgiveness.
From God's acceptance, not *for* His acceptance.
From God's approval, not *for* His approval.
From God's blessing, not *for* His blessing.
From God's love, not *for* His love.

Your middle school teacher was right. Prepositions matter. When it comes to prayer, *from* and *for* are worlds apart.

The premise of Jesus, Paul, and many others was that God was on their side. They believed they were accepted and loved and valuable to God, and those beliefs imbued their prayers, words, and actions with divine confidence.

Prayer helps establish and strengthen those same premises in us. When we pray, we affirm who we are in Christ and how much we mean to God. We see God's love in a deeper way. We discover His purposes for us. We grow in faith that His power will work through us.

Prayer done right will keep us in a place of healthy self-worth and godly self-confidence.

A positive view of self is vital. Dr. Albert Bandura, a psychologist who is highly regarded for his work on self-confidence, coined the term "self-efficacy" to describe our belief that we can (or can't) do something. I wrote about his theory in more detail in my book *Help! I Work with People*.

Based on his extensive research, Bandura said, "When beset with difficulties people who entertain serious doubts about their capabilities slacken their efforts or give up altogether, whereas those who have a strong sense of efficacy exert greater effort to master the challenges."[1]

In other words, what we believe we are capable of will determine how hard we work—or how quickly we give up when we face obstacles. Our brains have incredible power to motivate us or to demoralize us based on how we view ourselves.

Here's what you have to remember, though: Your opinion of who you are or what you can accomplish cannot be based solely on what *you* see and feel about yourself. And it definitely can't come only from what *others* say about you.

Your self-image must be grounded in what *God* says about you.

Yes, God knows all of our imperfections and mistakes, but He is not fixated on them. He doesn't shame us because of them. He's not up in heaven snickering with the angels at our failures, nor sitting around a war table scheduling our imminent judgment.

He has the opposite attitude. He is here to help, to serve, to make up for our lack. Our weaknesses make room for His strengths (2 Corinthians 12:9–10).

Your self-image must be grounded in what God says about you.

Jesus is proof that God's attitude toward us is one of love, not judgment, and that He treats us with acceptance, not shame.

Jesus described His mission this way: "For God did not send His Son into the world to condemn the world, but to save the world through him" (John 3:17). He spent three and a half years loving and serving everyone He came in contact with. He didn't condemn people for their mistakes. He offered them grace and forgiveness.

So if you find yourself avoiding prayer altogether, or if your prayers mostly consist of apologies, maybe you need to reevaluate your premises and perspectives about God. He's not your dentist. He's not your high school principal. He's not a cosmic police officer.

He's your father.

He's your friend.

He's your savior.

He's your protector.

He's your healer.

He's your confidante.

Pray and live from that reality.

PRAYERS AND PREMISES

Life too often reminds us of our insufficiencies: who we are not, what we lack, how far we still have to go.

Prayer, on the other hand, reminds us of the sufficiency of Christ. It helps us realize who we are in Him. It assures us that the blessings of heaven are ours. It reaffirms that God has brought us this far and isn't giving up on us now.

The Bible has a lot to say about the premises that underpin our relationship with God. I started to list a few of them, and I got a little carried away. I finally cut the list off at twenty-five.

1. *I am safe.*
   "Whoever dwells in the shelter of the Most High
   will rest in the shadow of the Almighty.
   I will say of the LORD, 'He is my refuge and my fortress,
   my God, in whom I trust.'"
   (Psalm 91:1–2)

2. *I am always on God's mind.*
   "How precious to me are your thoughts, God!
   How vast is the sum of them!
   Were I to count them,
   they would outnumber the grains of sand—
   when I awake, I am still with you."
   (Psalm 139:17–18)

3. *I am led by God.*
   "Trust in the LORD with all your heart
   and lean not on your own understanding;
   in all your ways submit to him,
   and he will make your paths straight."
   (Proverbs 3:5–6)

4. *I am at peace.*
   "You will keep in perfect peace
   all who trust in you,

46

all whose thoughts are fixed on you!"
(Isaiah 26:3 NLT)

5. *I am set free by the truth.*

"Jesus said, 'If you hold to my teaching, you are really my disciples. Then you will know the truth, and the truth will set you free. . . . So if the Son sets you free, you will be free indeed.'" (John 8:31–32, 36)

6. *I can hear God's voice.*

"My sheep listen to my voice; I know them, and they follow me." (John 10:27)

7. *I am a friend of God.*

"I no longer call you servants, because a servant does not know his master's business. Instead, I have called you friends, for everything that I learned from my Father I have made known to you." (John 15:15)

8. *I am chosen by God to bear fruit.*

"You did not choose me, but I chose you and appointed you so that you might go and bear fruit—fruit that will last—and so that whatever you ask in my name the Father will give you." (John 15:16)

9. *I am righteous.*

"Therefore, since we have been declared righteous by faith, we have peace with God through our Lord Jesus Christ." (Romans 5:1 NET)

10. *I am free from condemnation.*

"Therefore, there is now no condemnation for those who are in Christ Jesus." (Romans 8:1)

11. *I know everything is working together for my good.*

"And we know that in all things God works for the good of those who love him, who have been called according to his purpose." (Romans 8:28)

12. *I am more than a conqueror through God's love.*

"No, in all these things we are more than conquerors through him who loved us. For I am convinced that neither death nor life, neither angels nor demons, neither the present nor the future, nor any pow-ers, neither height nor depth, nor anything else in all creation, will be able to separate us from the love of God that is in Christ Jesus our Lord." (Romans 8:37–39)

13. *I am accepted.*

   "Accept one another, then, just as Christ accepted you, in order to bring praise to God." (Romans 15:7)

14. *I am stronger than sin or temptation.*

   "No temptation has overtaken you except what is common to mankind. And God is faithful; he will not let you be tempted beyond what you can bear. But when you are tempted, he will also provide a way out so that you can endure it." (1 Corinthians 10:13)

15. *I am part of the body of Christ.*

   "Now you are the body of Christ, and each one of you is a part of it." (1 Corinthians 12:27)

16. *I live by faith, and Jesus lives in me.*

   "I have been crucified with Christ and I no longer live, but Christ lives in me. The life I now live in the body, I live by faith in the Son of God, who loved me and gave himself for me." (Galatians 2:20)

17. *I am blessed.*

   "Praise be to the God and Father of our Lord Jesus Christ, who has blessed us in the heavenly realms with every spiritual blessing in Christ." (Ephesians 1:3)

18. *I am redeemed and forgiven.*

   "In him we have redemption through his blood, the forgiveness of sins, in accordance with the riches of God's grace." (Ephesians 1:7)

19. *I am God's handiwork, created to do good.*

   "For we are God's handiwork, created in Christ Jesus to do good works, which God prepared in advance for us to do." (Ephesians 2:10)

20. *I know God will finish the work He started in me.*

   "Being confident of this, that he who began a good work in you will carry it on to completion until the day of Christ Jesus." (Philippians 1:6)

21. *I am provided for by God.*

   "And my God will meet all your needs according to the riches of his glory in Christ Jesus." (Philippians 4:19)

22. *I am powerful, loving, and self-disciplined.*

   "For the Spirit God gave us does not make us timid, but gives us power, love and self-discipline." (2 Timothy 1:7)

23. *I have full access to the throne of grace.*

   "Let us then approach God's throne of grace with confidence, so that we may receive mercy and find grace to help us in our time of need." (Hebrews 4:16)

24. *I am a child of God.*

   "See what great love the Father has lavished on us, that we should be called children of God! And that is what we are!" (1 John 3:1)

25. *I am loved.*

   "This is how God showed his love among us: He sent his one and only Son into the world that we might live through him. This is love: not that we loved God, but that he loved us and sent his Son as an atoning sacrifice for our sins." (1 John 4:9–10)

If that list doesn't inspire you to pray with more confidence, I don't know what will! I could easily have listed another twenty-five statements about who we are in Christ and how God sees us. The Bible has so much to say about the premises for our prayers.

The next time you pray, take a few minutes to go through the list above. Get rid of the God-is-my-dentist mentality and trust that He is your friend, your Father, your Savior. Pray with a smile on your face, because when God hears your voice, He smiles too.

If you pray according to the Bible, you'll pray *from* the unshakeable premises of God's love, grace, and calling, not *for* them.

You'll be bold and confident and full of faith.

You'll ask for anything and pray about everything.

——————— FIVE ———————

I'd rather be at the beach

Prayer and perspective

I live in LA, which is famous for its beaches and its traffic. It's known for many other things too—street tacos, palm trees, movie stars . . . But beaches and traffic always top the list.

Can you imagine two more opposite experiences than reclining under an umbrella while you sip the drink of your choice on Malibu Beach, versus white-knuckling it through rush-hour traffic on a twelve-lane LA freeway? One inspires relaxation, gratitude, peace. The other makes you question your sanity.

There is something about the ocean that heals my soul. Not necessarily getting *into* the ocean. There are terrifying creatures in there that I'd prefer not to disturb. Plus, sand is . . . sandy.

But watching and listening to the ocean? That's my happy place.

The American poet e.e. cummings wrote, "It's always ourselves we find in the sea."[1]

The waves never stop. They roll in, one after the other, day after day, night after night, unbothered by the stress and chaos of the humans on land. Their rhythm is relaxing. Comforting. Grounding.

When you gaze out over the ocean, the sense of scale is awe-inspiring. Blue and green water dominates the view as far as you can see. And the expanse in front of you is just a tiny corner of a body of water that stretches around the globe, touching islands and continents you'll never visit. In the distance, where the sky meets the water, you see the horizon. It's a stable, unchanging line that is always there, even if it's obscured by passing storms.

Sometimes when I'm feeling stressed or overwhelmed, I'll go sit by the ocean just to reset my perspective. Julia and I have our favorite places. We know where we can avoid crowds, get good sushi, and let our kids play. It's glorious. I wish I was there now, to be honest.

I love this quote attributed to the Swedish environmentalist writer Rolf Edberg: "In still moments by the sea, life seems large—drawn and simple. It is there we can see into ourselves."[2]

I think he's talking about perspective. Life is big. We are small. Not everything matters as much as we think it does. And knowing who we are will bring us rest.

In many ways, prayer is like the ocean. It gives us perspective. It helps us place ourselves, ground ourselves, in the grand scheme of life.

You can't go to the beach or listen to the rhythm of the waves without realizing how big the world is. In the same way, you can't pray to an infinite God without finding yourself simultaneously comforted and awestruck by His greatness.

In the last chapter, we discussed the _premises_ that underlie our prayers: how we see God and ourselves. Now I'd like to look at how we see our circumstances. That's called _perspective_.

WORDS WITHOUT KNOWLEDGE

In the chaos and contradictions of life, prayer helps us gain a perspective that is bigger than our own.

There is an ancient book of poetry in the Bible called Job, named after its protagonist. Today, the story of Job is synonymous with suffering and patience. But in reality, Job's story is more about perspective than patience.

In chapters 1 and 2, we read how Job lost everything overnight. The text is clear that he wasn't to blame. Things outside his control conspired to take away everything he had worked for and valued.

The bulk of the book, chapters 3–37, is a series of poetic speeches or debates between Job and a few "comforters." These friends are supposedly trying to make Job feel better. As is often the case when we try to help people going through pain, they should have just kept their mouths shut and sat with him in his pain because what they said only made things worse.

By the end of their "advice," Job might have been suffering for days, weeks, or even months. His friends had exhausted themselves trying to explain why it was all Job's fault. He must have sinned, they argued, because (according to their theology and cosmology) bad things were always the consequences of bad actions. They defended God at the expense of Job. In the process, they actually undermined God's sovereignty and blamed Job for things he never did.

They had a wrong perspective: of Job, of suffering, of God, of sin, of wealth, and of just about everything else they pompously addressed. Their understanding made sense to them because they were looking at things from their limited, finite point of view. But God wasn't impressed by their theology or cosmology. He doesn't tend to appreciate humansplaining.

Finally, in chapters 38–41, God speaks. These chapters are some of the finest examples of ancient poetry, not just in the Bible, but in world literature. For four solid chapters, God blasts Job's friends for speaking "words without knowledge" (38:2). And He's not referring to Twitter.

God gives them example after example from nature that illustrates how small their perspective is, how limited their knowledge and power are. Speaking of oceans, God says this:

Who shut up the sea behind doors
    when it burst forth from the womb,
when I made the clouds its garment
    and wrapped it in thick darkness,
when I fixed limits for it
    and set its doors and bars in place,
when I said, "This far you may come and no farther;
    here is where your proud waves halt"?

Job 38:8–11

In other words, if you think the ocean is impressive, imagine the power of the one who created the ocean!

Now that's perspective!

When we go to God in prayer, He doesn't usually put us on blast quite as intensely as He did Job and his friends. For one thing, we (hopefully) don't spend so much time eloquently mouthing off about stuff we don't really understand.

What God does for us, and what prayer does for us, is provide perspective.

At those lunchtime prayer meetings at my high school, I remember watching kids leave the room with a completely different posture than when they had come in. They would tell us later how those fifteen minutes changed their outlook on what they were going through. They gained perspective.

I remember wandering the San Gabriel hills of LA, feeling both small and loved at the same time. That's perspective.

FROM DESPAIR TO DESTINY

Life (and traffic) have a way of skewing our perspective. Difficult, overwhelming circumstances can cause our emotions and thoughts to spiral out of control. I'm not saying those feelings and thoughts are not real. They absolutely are. But they are not the whole picture. And they aren't designed to make our decisions for us.

Which of these things have you felt lately? Or maybe even right now?

Lonely	Frustrated	Bitter
Betrayed	Discouraged	Anxious
Overwhelmed	Confused	Guilty
Useless	Rejected	Ignored
Hurt	Abandoned	Used
Lost	Hopeless	Powerless

Those feelings, if left unchecked, will affect your actions and decisions. You might find yourself doing or saying things that you later regret—things that don't align with who you are, what you value, what you believe, or how you want to live.

Again, the feelings are valid. Don't ignore them. But don't define yourself by them either. Don't let them tell you who you are. They are feelings, and feelings never give the whole picture. They come and go, they rise and fall, they make a lot of noise and then fade into the background.

There is a reason the book of Psalms is so emotionally charged. It's an ancient record of the heartfelt cries of people just like us. They turned their pain and anxiety into prayers, poetry, and songs. Their words resonate with us today, across the barriers of language, culture, and time, because their experiences are intensely *human*.

They are our experiences too.

Many of the psalms were written by David, a famous warrior, king, and musician in the Bible. One time, before David was king, he was living with a band of several hundred followers in the wilderness. While he and his men were away from the camp, marauders swooped in, kidnapped their families, and stole their livestock and goods.

When David and his men returned, they were shattered. The Bible says, "David and his men wept aloud until they had no strength left to weep" (1 Samuel 30:4).

It gets worse. David's men were so upset that, in their grief, they turned on David. Verse 6 says, "David was greatly distressed because the men were talking of stoning him; each one was bitter in spirit because of his sons and daughters."

Then we immediately read this amazing phrase: "But David found strength in the LORD his God."

David turned to prayer. Along with a priest named Abiathar, David asked God if he should go after the enemy army. God replied: "Pursue them. . . . You will certainly overtake them and succeed in the rescue" (verse 8).

That was all David needed. He returned to the crowd of devastated, angry men and told them the plan: They were going to get their families back. And they did. They recovered every last family member and all the livestock and goods that had been stolen.

How did David go from being "greatly distressed" to leading a daring rescue operation?

Prayer.

More specifically, prayer that changed his perspective. David connected with God, and God reminded him that he was not alone. God gave him direction about how to proceed. He instilled courage and faith in David's heart. That made all the difference.

Jesus did something similar in the garden of Gethsemane. He was hours away from being tortured and killed. He knew what was coming, and He was suffering—emotionally, mentally, and spiritually.

Luke wrote, "And being in anguish, he prayed more earnestly, and his sweat was like drops of blood falling to the ground" (22:44).

Notice the direct connection between His suffering and His prayer: "Being in anguish, he prayed more earnestly."

But first, He changes our perspective. And that changes everything.

In other words, the greater the pain, the more He prayed.

What if we did that? What if greater pain made us pray that much more? If greater anxiety carried us toward God?

I think it often does, actually. We automatically turn to prayer when we are at the end of ourselves. That's why David said, "From the ends of the earth I call to you, I call as my heart grows faint; lead me to the rock that is higher than I" (Psalm 61:2). He knew he needed a God who was bigger than him and stronger than him. And once he was standing upon that rock, his perspective shifted.

As I mentioned in chapter 3, God often turns our prayers back toward us. He tells us, like David when he had lost his family, to go back to the fight.

But first, He changes our perspective. And that changes everything.

THROUGH GOD'S EYES

It's God's prerogative to shift our perspective in any area, but there are a few areas that seem especially common.

1. Self

We looked at this in detail in the last chapter. You need to see yourself as God sees you. Period. No more, no less. That is the path to both true humility and healthy self-esteem.

As you pray, let God shift the way you think about yourself. Believe His affirmations of who you are. Then align the way you talk about yourself, and present yourself with that image

2. Pain

Too often we are in such a hurry to fix pain that we either suppress it or offer it cheap solutions, much like Job's friends.

Prayer does neither of those.

Prayer doesn't dismiss pain. It embraces it. Validates it. Sits with it.

It creates a safe space to process what we are feeling, and it connects us to the one who can truly make a difference in our circumstances. It gives us permission to express our feelings while also affirming that this too shall pass.

Prayer might not eliminate pain, but it reminds us that God is with us. Because of that reality, we can walk through the valley of the shadow of death and fear no evil (see Psalm 23).

3. Sin

Sin is anything that contradicts God's will and design for us. We tend to either fixate on it and make escaping sin the focus of our Christian walk, or we minimize it so that we don't have to address some area of our lives.

Both extremes are wrong, of course. Following Jesus is about freedom and life and grace and love—not about "not sinning." Not sinning is a byproduct of following Jesus; it's not the point.

On the other hand, prayer keeps you honest. When you are in God's presence, hidden motivations are revealed. Dark corners are illuminated. Inner demons are exposed and evicted. The result is a clean heart and a healthy hatred of sin.

4. Enemies

God is not nearly as intimidated by opposition as we are. Not at all intimidated, in fact. The Bible is full of examples of God giving His people victory.

But Jesus takes it a step further. He tells us to *love* our enemies. Talk about a different perspective.

> You have heard that it was said, "Love your neighbor and hate your enemy." But I tell you, love your enemies and pray for those who persecute you, that you may be children of your Father in heaven. He causes his sun to rise on the evil and the good, and sends rain on the righteous and the unrighteous.
>
> Matthew 5:43–45

Jesus didn't just tell us to love your enemies. He did it. While hanging on the cross they were crucifying Him upon, He said, "Father, forgive them, for they do not know what they are doing" (Luke 23:34).

5. Obstacles

One time, Jesus and His disciples were crossing a large lake called the Sea of Galilee, and they were overtaken by a storm. Several of the disciples were experienced fishermen, but this storm was so bad they were afraid they were going to drown.

Mark recounts that Jesus was asleep in the back, peacefully resting on a pillow while His disciples nearly lost their minds. Finally, they woke Him up. "Teacher, don't you care if we drown?" (4:38).

Jesus woke up, yawned, stretched, looked around, yawned again, then casually told the wind and the waves to knock it off.

Instant calm.

The disciples, Mark writes, were now terrified of *Him*, not the storm. In a good way. "Who is this? Even the wind and the waves obey him!" (verse 41).

They had a perspective change. Rather than being in awe of the elements, they were in awe of the one who created and controlled the wind and the waves.

Prayer reminds us that all obstacles are small next to the omnipotent creator of the universe.

6. Material things

We invest so much of ourselves trying to make money and build wealth. But the one who dies with the most toys . . . still dies.

Maybe you've heard the Biggie Smalls song "Juicy." I know I'm dating myself here, since it first came out in 1994, but it's a classic, and it's one of the greatest hip-hop songs of all time. It's about Biggie's rags-to-riches journey, and it's mostly an in-your-face message to the haters who never thought he'd make it.

There are so many great lines in the song that point out just how far he had come, like, "Now we sip champagne when we thirsty."[3]

That's what we've all been taught, right? That success looks like fancy cars and tastes like champagne?

But with all due respect to the late Christopher Wallace, that kind of success can't bring lasting contentment. It beats poverty, for sure—but we have to get our perspective on success from God, not from rap artists.

Prayer gives us perspective on money and success because it brings heavenly values to bear on our earthly pursuits. It reminds us that what lasts longer is what is worth the most. And what lasts the longest is what is eternal.

Mostly, that means *people*. Material things don't go to heaven, but people do. That doesn't mean you shouldn't care about your job, house, car, or espresso machine. It just means you should care more about people.

7. People

People matter more than anything, and praying for individuals in your life will always change your perspective about them. This might mean praying for your enemies, as we saw above. But more often, it means praying for friends and loved ones.

Every relationship in your life could benefit from prayer. Are you dating someone? Pray for your significant other. Are you recently married? Pray for your spouse. Are you a parent? Pray for your kids. Are you a boss? Pray for your employees. Are you a pet owner? Okay, pray for your pets too. Are you a basketball fan? Unless you root for the Lakers, don't bother praying.

In prayer, you'll start to see others the way God does. The quirks and petty offenses will matter less, and their innate value as children of God will take center place. You'll start to see their gifts, their contributions, their potential.

As you take on God's perspective toward people, you'll find yourself developing empathy. Prayer humanizes people. This world could certainly use more of that.

Besides those seven things, you can probably think of other areas where a heavenly perspective would be helpful: health, school, work, family, sex, world affairs, racism, leadership, church, and a million things more.

You won't change your world until you change your mind.

Besides these general areas, maybe there are specific situations in your life where you could ask God to see things with His eyes. Take a few moments to think through the things that are worrying you, draining your energy, or causing pain.

Then pray about them. Give them to God. Ask Him what He thinks about them. Allow the mind of Christ to become your mind. Let His heart touch your heart.

You won't change your world until you change your mind.

The problem with birthdays

Prayer and presence

Do you have friends who have more money than you? Like, considerably more? No judgment here, either for them or for you. We all know money doesn't make us happy. (Although it would be nice to prove that firsthand, right?)

A couple of my friends are significantly wealthier than I am. And I sort of dread their birthdays. After all, what do you get the person who has two of three of everything, in different colors?

Every year, after giving the question deep thought, I give up. I settle for a text message. "Bro, happy birthday! Love you! Let's celebrate ASAP!"

And then I pray to the God of heaven that they don't buy *me* anything for my birthday.

My wealthy friends don't need my gifts. They don't want me to blow up my budget by trying to impress them either. They want my friendship, not gifts. That's what matters most to them, and it's what matters most to me.

It's hard enough to buy gifts for the friends who have everything. But what do you give the *God* who has everything?

God isn't trying to get something *from* you—He is trying to get *you*.

The answer, of course, is the same. You give Him your friendship. Your love. Your loyalty. Your presence.

God isn't trying to get something *from* you—He is trying to get *you*. You are the gift. You are the goal. You are the object of His love.

Jesus proved that when He came to earth to walk among us, to show us God with skin on, and to draw us close to Him. God's greatest delight is to be with you and me, with us, His children. And we have a need hardwired into our soul to be with Him.

Amid the worries and the hustle of life, we sometimes forget the healing power of simply being with God. When we sense His closeness, everything changes. Our fears fade away, our minds clear, our hearts become calm.

THE FELT PRESENCE OF GOD

The idea of God's presence is found throughout the Bible. God is, of course always present. He's omnipresent, meaning He is everywhere, all the time.

Paul, writing about Jesus, says, "He is before all things, and in him all things hold together" (Colossians 1:17). God is the life-force that keeps the universe humming.

On a more personal level, the author of Hebrews, speaking for God, says, "Never will I leave you; never will I forsake you" (13:5). God doesn't just hold all of creation together; He holds us in His arms. He remains with us no matter what.

God's presence in the universe and in our lives never changes. But there is another element of His presence that we find in the Bible and in our walk with Him. It's His "felt presence," for lack of a better term. It's that sudden, unexplainable, thrilling awareness that He is, quite literally, in the room.

You can't explain it.

It might include emotion, but it's deeper than any human feeling.

It might cause goosebumps or tears or laugher, but it's more than superficial reactions.

It might be specific words or thoughts that drop into your heart, but it goes beyond mere imagination.

You just know that God showed up. And His presence changes everything.

Prayer facilitates this felt presence of God. It opens your mind and spirit to receive from God.

I'm not saying you'll have some dramatic experience every time you pray, but you'll often feel or sense something. You should expect it, look for it, and welcome it. Don't make experience the goal of prayer, but don't reduce prayer to a mental exercise either.

Prayer is both an act of faith and an experience.

It is both words and emotions.

It is both talking and listening.

It is mind and spirit and will and body together, experiencing God in a tangible way.

God can show up whenever and however He wants. He loves to interact with us. He wants to be found by us. As He told Israel, "You will seek me and find me when you seek me with all your heart" (Jeremiah 29:13).

He's here with us all the time, after all, and He loves us deeply—doesn't it make sense that He would want to reveal himself to us? Speak to us? Comfort us? Lead us?

Moses conversed with God in front of a burning bush and again on a mountaintop. (Exodus 3–4; 33)

Israel experienced God's presence in a pillar of fire and cloud. (Exodus 13:21–22)

Deborah received marching orders from God and delivered Israel. (Judges 4–5)

Solomon consecrated the temple and God's glory filled it. (2 Chronicles 5–7)

Elijah heard God's voice as a whisper while he was hiding in a cave. (1 Kings 19:12–13)

Daniel was accompanied by an angel, who shut the mouth of lions. (Daniel 6:22)

Shadrach, Meshach, and Abednego were joined by God in the fiery furnace. (Daniel 3)

Mary was visited by an angel announcing the birth of Jesus. (Luke 1:26–38)

Peter, James, and John saw Jesus transfigured and glorious on a mountain. (Matthew 17:1–2)

Mary Magdalene encountered Jesus in a garden the morning of the resurrection. (John 20)

Paul was knocked to the ground and his life changed on the way to Jerusalem. (Acts 9)

John had a series of apocalyptic dreams that reveal God's ultimate victory. (Revelation)

I could go on, but you get the picture. God has a long history of visiting humanity in very creative ways. And He hasn't stopped.

Apparently, He likes being with us.

CHOOSING WHAT IS BETTER

In the chaos and craziness and pain and pressure of life, prayer helps us slow down. It creates a space for us to listen to God's voice.

One day, Jesus stopped by the house of two sisters named Mary and Martha. This is probably the same Mary and Martha whose brother Lazarus was later raised from the dead by Jesus. Luke tells us that Mary "sat at the Lord's feet listening to what he said" (10:39). Martha, on the other hand, was "distracted by all the preparations that had to be made" (verse 40).

Martha needed help in the kitchen, and she expected Mary to do her part. I can imagine Martha gesturing to Mary when Jesus wasn't watching. Coughing and sighing loudly from the kitchen. Whispering menacingly into Mary's ear. Dropping passive-aggressive hints every time she hurried in with another bowl of snacks about "how hot it is in the kitchen" and "how much work there is left to do."

Mary blissfully ignored her.

At some point, Martha couldn't take it anymore, and she lost it. She complained to Jesus: "Lord, don't you care that my sister has left me to do the work by myself? Tell her to help me!" (verse 40).

Gently but firmly, Jesus refused.

"Martha, Martha," the Lord answered, "you are worried and upset about many things, but few things are needed—or indeed only one. Mary has chosen what is better, and it will not be taken away from her" (verses 41–42).

Notice the two postures contrasted here: _sitting_ versus _serving_. Sitting at a teacher's feet was the customary place of a disciple. By the way, this contradicted gender norms of the day, which usually said only men could be disciples. Women should be where Martha was—in the kitchen, in the background, unseen and unheard.

There's nothing wrong with serving in the background, of course. Jesus had a lot to say about serving. It's a good thing and we should do _more_ of it, not less. But serving should never replace being in God's presence. And it definitely shouldn't be imposed upon someone based on gender or some other cultural stereotype.

Mary didn't let gender norms, family expectations, to-do lists, or even smoke pouring from the kitchen stop her. She wanted to be with Jesus. So she ignored everything else, sat down, and listened. Period.

I don't want the sum of my life to be my résumé. I want it be relationships. First with God, second with my family, and third with my friends and others in my life.

She didn't let good things distract her from the best thing.

Martha, on the other hand, was busy. Not just occupied, but genuinely stressed out. Anxious, worried, upset, distracted, overwhelmed, frantic, pressured.

That sounds a lot like our culture today. There is always more to do than there is time to do it. We are always running, eternally working, constantly distracted. We flaunt our busyness like a merit badge, as if being forever busy is proof of our importance.

But what if being forever busy is simply proof that we don't have our priorities right?

Not too long ago, while on vacation, I read *The Ruthless Elimination of Hurry* by John Mark Comer. It wrecked me in a good way. He argues that busyness is one of the greatest enemies of spirituality. He says this:

> Because *what you give your attention to is the person you become.* Put another way: the mind is the portal to the soul, and what you fill your mind with will shape the trajectory of your character. In the end, your life is no more than the sum of what you gave your attention to.[1]

I don't want the sum of my life to be my résumé. I want it be relationships. First with God, second with my family, and third with my friends and others in my life.

There is a place for working hard, setting goals, and using time effectively. I'll be the first to say that. I love dreaming big and then striving to achieve those dreams. Seeing tangible results thrills me.

But there is also a place for setting down the phone, turning off the laptop, and tuning in to God and people around us. We need to learn how to be present in the moment.

That is exactly what prayer does for us. It seats us at the feet of Jesus. We listen to Him and learn from Him, we grow closer to Him, even if that means lunch is a bit delayed.

When you already have too much to do, it feels counterintuitive to do nothing. To sit in the presence of God and listen. But choosing to be with Jesus is choosing "what is better," to quote Him.

Don't let anyone take that away from you.

THE GIFT OF HIS PRESENCE

Typically, when we pray, we are looking for answers. But His presence is the greatest gift. It's better than any miracle. Our circumstances might remain the same, our hearts might still be hurting, our problems might not be resolved—and yet, simply knowing He is with us is enough.

What do we receive in His presence?

1. Joy

David wrote:

> You make known to me the path of life;
> you will fill me with joy in your presence,
> with eternal pleasures at your right hand.
> Psalm 16:11

Joy supersedes circumstances. You can be joyful even when you are going through difficult times. That doesn't mean you ignore your pain, but it means that God's presence fills you with a joy that is deeper, wider, and more permanent than the situation you are facing.

2. Peace

I quoted this earlier, but it's worth mentioning again in the context of God's presence:

> You will keep in perfect peace
> all who trust in you,
> all whose thoughts are fixed on you!
>
> Isaiah 26:3 NLT

When God shows up in your prayer time, you know that things will work out. It will be okay. This circumstance, tragedy, pain, or trial will pass. Even though the storm rages around you, you know you are safe.

3. Wisdom

The apostle James wrote, "If any of you lacks wisdom, you should ask God, who gives generously to all without finding fault, and it will be given to you" (James 1:5).

God's presence brings clarity. You might not see the whole plan, but you at least see the next step. His presence enables you to sort through the complex emotions and thoughts that vie for your attention and to make sane, healthy choices.

4. Courage

When Joshua took over the leadership of Israel from Moses, he had big sandals to fill. He also had an impossible task in front of him: leading Israel into the Promised Land.

God said to him, "This is my command—be strong and courageous! Do not be afraid or discouraged. For the LORD your God is with you wherever you go" (Joshua 1:9 NLT).

Joshua probably thought he needed strategies, weapons, and warriors. But God said he needed *courage* and he needed God's *presence*. And those two things were connected.

5. Understanding

Earlier I mentioned that Jesus raised Lazarus, the brother of Mary and Martha, from the dead. Before He performed the miracle, though, He talked with Mary and Martha. He listened to them. He heard their pain and saw their grief.

And then He wept (John 11:35).

Even though He was God, even though He knew the pain would soon end, He felt empathy and compassion. He didn't dismiss their pain; He sat with it. He sat with them.

I'm sure Mary and Martha had never felt so seen and heard as they did that day.

When you pray, God sees you and hears you. His presence accompanies you and comforts you. He laments with you. He celebrates with you. He does life with you.

6. Rest

Earlier I quoted Jesus' invitation to the multitudes: "Come to me, all you who are weary and burdened, and I will give you rest. Take my yoke upon you and learn from me, for I am gentle and humble in heart, and you will find rest for your souls" (Matthew 11:28–29).

When we draw near to God, we find rest for our souls. I think that's what Mary found, and it's what Martha needed.

Don't be in a hurry to leave His presence. Sit at His feet for a while, enjoying His favor and His gaze. Let busyness dissolve and time stand still. Nothing matters more than being with Him.

Joy, peace, wisdom, courage, understanding, rest—God's presence gives us all of that and more. But ultimately, it's less about what we get and more about who we are with. The benefits are secondary to His presence.

God himself is His gift to us. And we are our gift to Him.

So, once again, what do you give a God who has everything?

You.

You give Him you.

SEVEN

Have you tried resetting it?

Prayer and process

When your phone, computer, or Wi-Fi router starts giving you trouble, the first line of defense is always the same.

Reset it.

That simply means that you turn it off, turn it back on, and hope for the best. If the mouse is stuck, you reboot your computer. If Candy Crush is lagging, you restart your phone. If the router appears to have given up the ghost, you reset it.

It doesn't matter what device it is or what is going wrong, you reset the thing.

No one really knows what happens inside the device when you reset it. I guess it cleans out fragmented files or unused pieces of . . . something. I don't know. Demons, maybe.

The point is, it usually works when you reset it. And when a device that two minutes earlier seemed to be gasping on its deathbed suddenly springs back to life, it restores your faith in technology.

Of course, if you have forty-seven unsaved documents open on your laptop, shutting it down is the last thing you want to do. But if you keep going and ignore the warning signs, sooner or later, it freezes up completely. Then you find yourself desperately hoping that you didn't lose everything.

Unfortunately, kids don't have an actual reset button, but sleep accomplishes a similar function. When they are falling apart mentally and emotionally, Julia and I just look at each other and count down the hours until bedtime. Then we hope that the fragmented thoughts or demons or whatever is rattling around inside their heads get cleared out by morning.

Side note: It's even harder to shut down a kid at night than to shut down your word processor and forty-seven documents.

I'm straying from the topic. Complaining about parenting is therapeutic, though, so thank you for listening. You can send me your bill.

Prayer is a bit like resetting your soul. And just as with computers and small children, how exactly it helps can seem like a bit of a mystery. God's ways are higher than our ways, after all.

I know that when I pray, it settles and focuses my mind. It clears out some of those fragmented things—thoughts, projects, hurt, sin, emotions, challenges, plans—that rattle around in my soul. It definitely helps expel a few inner demons.

Spending a few minutes in prayer refreshes us on the inside. It gives us a clean start and a new beginning. Prayer helps us process the things we have on our hearts and in our brains. In a sense, prayer is like going through those unsaved documents, deciding whether to save them or delete them or finish them, then closing them down and clearing up some headspace.

Spending a few minutes in prayer refreshes us on the inside.

There is a lot of pain, confusion, and trauma in life, but the Holy Spirit helps us work through those things. He gives us understanding into what matters and what doesn't, what can be discarded and what we should hold on to.

72

DEAR GOD, ARE YOU SERIOUS?

Being able to process our pain, doubts, and trauma in God's presence is part of an emotionally healthy spiritual walk. It's also something that God-followers have done for thousands of years. Just look at the book of Psalms.

David was an incredible example of someone who knew how to take things to God in prayer. When you read his psalms, you often see a progression that looks something like this:

1. Pain: complaint, suffering, sorrow
2. Processing: struggling with the contradictions
3. Prayer: turning to God for help
4. Proclamation: affirming faith and trust in God
5. Peace: settled, calm, and expectant

In other words, his prayers—just like ours—were dynamic. He learned and grew as he prayed.

You don't pray from a place of perfection. Your prayers are not carefully crafted, emotionless, self-controlled speeches to God.

They come from the heart.

If they don't, they aren't really prayer.

You pray from a place of need, trust, humility, and even desperation. And as you pray through your circumstances, you find something happening on the inside.

You change. You learn. You grow.

And eventually, you reset. You sort through the fragmented thoughts that were holding you back. You work through the emotions that were taking so much of your focus. You find yourself once again full of faith and courage.

This five-point progression isn't a formula to follow, but rather an illustration of the dynamic nature of prayer. Let's look at Psalm 22 as an example.

1. Pain: complaint, suffering, sorrow

David starts by expressing his pain and feelings of abandonment:

> My God, my God, why have you forsaken me?
> Why are you so far from saving me,
> so far from my cries of anguish?
> My God, I cry out by day, but you do not answer,
> by night, but I find no rest.
>
> verses 1–2

You might recognize that first line. Jesus quoted it on the cross. Actually, much of this psalm parallels Jesus' suffering on the cross, and all four gospels refer back to it when describing His crucifixion.

Both David and Jesus expressed their pain honestly. They didn't try to put on some spiritual mask, pretending things were okay. They cried out. They expressed their emotions.

The best prayers are real prayers. They aren't eloquent, but they are heartfelt. They aren't polished, but they are transparent. They aren't theological masterpieces, but they touch the heart of God.

Dear God, like, really?

Dear God, are you serious?

Dear God, where in the world are you?

Dear God, I'm done. I'm at the end of my rope.

God isn't scandalized by that level of honesty. He won't get His feelings hurt over it. That is exactly how the psalmist prayed, time after time.

God already knows our hearts, so why not be transparent with Him? We can tell Him that we feel alone, betrayed, abandoned, afraid, angry, disappointed, confused, or hurt.

Maybe you've been told that is disrespectful, but God calls it honest.

2. Processing: struggling with the contradictions

David doesn't stay in that dark place, though. He processes his feelings by turning to God. He starts by saying this:

> Yet you are enthroned as the Holy One;
> you are the one Israel praises.
> In you our ancestors put their trust;
> they trusted and you delivered them.
> To you they cried out and were saved;
> in you they trusted and were not put to shame.
>
> verses 3–5

What is David doing? He is remembering God's works in the past. He is reminding himself that God has always been faithful, and He won't stop now.

Part of processing our pain is to ground our present circumstances in the bigger picture. Pain has a way of shouting so urgently that we think the entire sky is falling. But maybe it's just a small piece of it. Or an acorn. The only way to know is to spend some time reflecting on who God is, what He has done for us, how great He is, and where we fit in His plan.

After that moment of light, though, things grow dark again. David poetically laments how powerless he feels. It's like the clouds of doubt cleared for a moment, then closed in on him again.

A couple verses later, there's another change. David affirms his own journey of trust in God.

> Yet you brought me out of the womb;
> you made me trust in you, even at my mother's breast.
> From birth I was cast on you;
> from my mother's womb you have been my God.
>
> verses 9–10

David recognizes that he has always trusted God. Sure, there have been moments where he hasn't felt very confident, but over his lifetime, he has walked by faith. God is his God, and David trusts Him.

If it feels like some emotional whiplash is happening here, that's because it is. We are getting a real-time, live-streamed view of David's emotional, mental, and spiritual journey.

And it sounds a lot like ours, if we're honest.

Prayer doesn't "fix" our emotions or thoughts immediately. Fixing them isn't even the goal because they aren't broken in the first place. They are part of who we are, part of the journey we are on.

When you're praying, don't hide from the roller coaster of feelings. Sometimes your prayers get darker before they get lighter.

God is not afraid of strong emotion.

He created all the feels, and He feels them all with us.

3. Prayer: turning to God for help

After David affirms his trust in God, he begins to offer up a heartfelt prayer for help.

> Do not be far from me,
> for trouble is near
> and there is no one to help.
>
> verse 11

He spends a solid eleven verses asking God for deliverance. This is the heart of the prayer in many ways, but it took him a while to get here. He had to let God deal with the convoluted emotions that were screaming for attention first.

Again, it's poetry, so you probably won't be quite so eloquent when you're praying. That's fine. Prayer is talking to God about what you hope, need, expect, want, or dream about. Remember, just be honest.

4. Proclamation: affirming faith and trust in God

By the time he's done expressing his request to God, David seems like an entirely new man. Listen to his triumphant language:

> I will declare your name to my people;
> in the assembly I will praise you.
> You who fear the LORD, praise him!
> All you descendants of Jacob, honor him!
> Revere him, all you descendants of Israel!
> For he has not despised or scorned
> the suffering of the afflicted one;
> He has not hidden his face from him
> but has listened to his cry for help.
>
> verses 22–24

Not only is David now announcing to the world how awesome God is, he even declares that God has *not* ignored or abandoned him—the exact opposite of how he started this psalm.

5. Peace: settled, calm, and expectant

David spends several more verses talking about God's power, faithfulness, and love.

By the end of the psalm, he is in a completely different headspace and heartspace than when he began. He is confident and full of faith, with peace in his soul.

That doesn't mean anything changed in the outside world, but everything had changed in his inside world. That was what mattered most.

These five things—pain, processing, prayer, proclamation, peace—are intuitive parts of prayer. They don't always happen in this order, and they are often cyclical, not linear: you cry out, then you ask for help, then you come to a place of trust and rest . . . and then another wave of pain crashes over you, and the cycle repeats. But with each cycle, you find more stability and peace, like an upward spiral out of the depths.

Again, your prayers don't have to follow this pattern. They definitely don't have to include so many metaphors and poetic language. But they will almost always involve some sort of process, some sort of progression. You'll come out on the other side with greater clarity and strength than before.

EMOTIONALLY HEALTHY PRAYERS

Peter Scazzero writes in his book *Emotionally Healthy Spirituality*, "Christian spirituality, without an integration of emotional health, can be deadly—to yourself, your relationship with God, and the people around you."[1]

He's right. It's not enough to just have faith or to pursue holiness or to study theology. We also have to be healthy on the inside, particularly in regard to our emotions.

We are wholistic beings: body, soul, and spirit. Mind, will, and emotions. If one part of our self is hurting, sooner or later it will affect the others.

Sometimes Christians are the worst at admitting emotional needs. We tend to think that faith means always being up and never being down. We don't give ourselves space to grieve, to emote, to vent, to rage, to hurt, to cry.

Life has a lot of trauma, though. If we don't process that trauma, it can deposit layers of hurt in our souls. We often create defense mechanisms or survival techniques just to keep it all together.

But deep inside, we are not in a good place.

And God knows it.

Here's the thing, though: He's not disappointed in us; He just wants to help us.

We must learn to take those difficult, dark things to God in prayer. Things like pain. Guilt. Fear. Shame. Anger. Betrayal. Addictions. Abuse. Trauma.

I'm sure you've had your fair share of seasons like those. Maybe you're in one right now. Learn to process your feelings in prayer. To sit with them and to sit with God at the same time, allowing Him to walk you through the hidden recesses of your heart and bring healing.

Side note: You might want to try writing out your prayers. I do that sometimes, and it can be so clarifying.

The act of putting pain into words can be healing itself, but it also allows us to unpack what we feel, to deconstruct it and look at it more objectively. Maybe that's why David wrote so many psalms. He was working through some pretty major trauma, and we get to peek into his process.

As I mentioned in chapter 1, prayer doesn't replace other ways of dealing with pain and trauma. Utilize the wisdom and science humanity has discovered. Truth is universal and ultimately comes from God. So I'm not saying you shouldn't turn to human sources for help. After all, God usually answers our prayers for help by sending humans.

But you do have a relationship with God—a direct line to heaven. Through prayer, you can receive help directly from Him.

Nobody in your life knows you as well as God does. And none of them are as capable of carrying your emotional pain as God is. If you turn to humans for what only God can provide, you'll likely end up burning them out and disillusioning yourself.

He's with you always. Turn to Him first, most, and last.

If you're going to therapy, keep going. But try praying before and afterward. If you're finding help in some other way, don't stop. Keep reading, keep learning, keep talking, keep taking care of yourself, keep creating boundaries, keep building better friendships, keep taking your medication, keep journaling, keep living in the moment . . . you get the idea.

Just add prayer to what you're already doing.

God wants to come alongside you in the process. He wants to help you reset, reboot, and restart, to work through the fragmented files and the demons, the dreams and the traumas, the ups and down and ins and outs of this complex human experience we call life.

He's with you always. Turn to Him first, most, and last.

EIGHT

Growing pains

Prayer and Perfection

My wife is a bit of a perfectionist. In a good way, of course. She's an Enneagram type 1 all the way: hard worker, driven to fix what is not working, internally compelled to get things done—and done right. I love it. (A big shout out to all the Enneagram lovers out there. In my opinion it's basically the Christian horoscope, but hey, who am I to judge?)

I, on the other hand, am not a perfectionist. However, I am obsessive-compulsive in certain areas. It's sort of a selective perfectionism. There are particular things that must be in order and in line: the lawn, the flower bed, the furniture, my notes for a message, my clothes . . .

I'm particularly obsessed with wrinkles. Specifically, with eliminating them. I have been passionate about ironing since at least 1999. When I first started in ministry, we had to wear a full suit to church every Sunday. Hence, my love for ironing. Even now, with the more relaxed culture, I still get my entire outfit ready the night before: pants and shirt chosen, ironed, and laid out in pristine condition. The next day, during the entire drive to church, I hold my seat belt in my hand, away from my shirt, to preserve that soothing smoothness for as long as possible.

Perfection, of course, is impossible on this planet. At least the way we tend to look at it.

In the Bible, the Greek word often translated "perfect" is *teleios*. It refers to something that is whole, complete, or finished; it can fulfill its purpose because it has all it needs.[1]

That's a very different understanding of the word *perfect* than you or I might have.

We tend to associate perfection with achieving some ideal state of excellence, performance, or morality. Something that is perfect, in our minds, does not need to change because it doesn't have any flaws. Perfectionists are people who strive for perfection in every area.

The Bible concept of being perfect, though, is less about striving toward some impossible ideal and more about *maturity*. It's the idea of becoming more complete, more congruent with the design and purpose God has for us.

It's about becoming more *you*.

Perfection, therefore, is less about the goal and more about the process. It is about *growth*.

Think of how your physical body grew when you were a kid. You couldn't see the growth, you couldn't predict the growth, and you couldn't really control the growth. It just happened. And it was unstoppable.

Spiritual growth is similar: slow, natural, inevitable, unstoppable.

Remember, our spiritual growth (including sinning less) isn't connected to our salvation. Salvation is a gift from God by grace. We don't go to church, pray, worship, fast, avoid sin, love our neighbor, or help the poor in order to be forgiven by God.

Rather, we do these things *because* we are forgiven. It's the whole "from-not-for" dynamic we talked about earlier. We are free to do good things; and as we do them, we grow in our walk with God.

We begin to think, speak, and act more like Jesus. That's true perfection.

We see the word *teleion* multiple times in the book of James. For example, he writes:

> Consider it all joy, my brothers and sisters, when you encounter various trials, knowing that the testing of your faith produces endurance. And let endurance have its *perfect* result, so that you may be *perfect* and complete, lacking in nothing.
>
> 1:2–4 NASB, emphasis added

To be honest, I'm not too excited about the emphasis here on *trials*. I'd rather avoid troubles, tests, and trials. Wouldn't you?

And yet, James reminds us that they play an important part in our spiritual growth. He tells us that going through tough things builds endurance, and endurance will have a "perfect result," which includes making us "perfect and complete."

Perfection is a process—and not an easy one. It's something that happens as we walk with God and allow Him to change us.

In high school, I had a friend who grew seven inches in one summer: from six foot two to six foot nine. His name was Brannon, and he was an incredible basketball player. You know what I remember him talking about a lot?

Growing pains.

Everybody wants to grow, but nobody wants to hurt. And yet, the two are often connected. But here's the thing:

Growing *pains* are temporary, but *growth* is permanent.

We can embrace the awkwardness and discomfort of the growth process because we know we are going to love the result.

PRAY THROUGH THE PROCESS

What does all this have to do with prayer?

Trials don't produce change overnight. Tests don't automatically make us complete and perfect. We have to *go through them*. That's where prayer comes in. Prayer is our connection to God in the midst of trials.

Prayer changes *us*. Yes, prayer changes things around us. But mostly, it transforms you and me.

Prayer connects our faith to our actions. It keeps us honest before God and open to the correction of the Holy Spirit. It leads us toward perfection, toward completeness.

When we pray, we grow.

Prayer is not the only way for us to grow, of course. Reading the Bible, being in a church community, worship, talking with other people, classes, experience, getting counsel, and more all contribute to being well-rounded humans.

Prayer is our connection to God in the midst of trials.

There is something unique about prayer, though, especially when we are going through difficult times. So often we turn to prayer in an attempt to *get out* of tough times. When that doesn't work, we pray to *get through* tough times.

But what about praying to *grow through* those times? What if God wants to respond to our prayers by causing us to be bigger, more complete, more mature people?

I think that's exactly what often happens.

It's no coincidence that James talks about personal growth in the context of trials and endurance. I wish it weren't this way, but we tend to grow when we are forced to do so. Some trial, some test, or some trouble comes our way, and in order to face it, we have to develop new abilities or tools.

That's a good thing! Why *go through* when you can *grow through*?

As we think about character perfection (aka completeness or maturity) and what prayer has to do with it, there are a few things to keep in mind.

1. Growth takes work.

Personal growth is rarely easy or fun. It's more often described with words like *uncomfortable, painful, slow, scary, laborious, humbling,* and *confusing.*

And yet, the results are worth it.

When I played high school basketball, we all loved the games, but nobody loved drills. Nobody enjoyed running laps. Nobody showed up to practice excited about being yelled at by sadistic coaches who spent their free time dreaming up ways to drive us to exhaustion.

Come game time, though, we were glad for every minute we had invested in our development. The pain was temporary, but the results were obvious. We had built endurance. We had developed our skills and our potential. We had become complete players.

That was a long time ago. These days I play "for fun," which is another way of saying none of us are going to work too hard at it. No coach is yelling at us to run laps. We don't do drills. There are no weight goals or diet restrictions. Just a bunch of guys with dad bods showing up, talking smack, and trying not to pull any muscles.

It is fun, for sure. But if anyone were to scout our pickup games (which will never happen), words like *endurance, skilled,* and *complete* would be absent from their clipboards.

If you're going to grow, you have to put in the work. And *prayer* is a big part of the work.

Pray through your trials.

Pray through your challenges.

Pray through your doubts and fears.

Pray through your screwups.

Pray through your frustrations.

Pray through your character flaws.

Pray through your lack.

Pray through your business ideas.

Pray through your options.

The more you pray about these things, the more God will speak to you and change you. I love this prayer that David wrote:

> Search me, God, and know my heart;
> test me and know my anxious thoughts.
> See if there is any offensive way in me,
> and lead me in the way everlasting.
>
> Psalm 139:23–24

David didn't arrogantly assume he was right in everything. He knew he might have blind spots, ulterior motives, toxic thinking, or offensive behavior. So he submitted his heart to God in prayer.

God will take you up on that prayer, by the way. I'll talk more about that later, in a chapter called "These are dangerous prayers." So only pray if you're serious about growth.

Trials will change you, if you let them. They'll make you a better, more perfect version of yourself. It might take some blood, sweat, and tears, but the results are worth it.

2. Growth takes time.

It takes your whole life, to be precise. I don't mean that to sound discouraging—what I'm saying is that you will continue to grow for as long as you're walking this planet. Growth is natural. It's healthy. And it never stops.

Many of us have the false assumption about growth that someday, if we try really hard, we will reach the pinnacle of perfection and never have to change again. That is not going to happen this side of heaven.

This is why prayer is such a vital tool. It keeps the lines of communication permanently open with God. Not just during a one-time emergency, but all the time.

Sometimes we treat prayer like a tech support request. Have you ever submitted one of those? Maybe you can't figure out why a program or service you paid for isn't working, so you contact their support team. They open a case for you, help you solve the problem (if you're lucky), then close the case. You get a nice email at the end summarizing how helpful they've been. And you never speak again. The entire thing is cold, faceless, voiceless.

That's not the point of prayer, though. Prayer is so much more than formally requesting help for a problem you can't figure out. The Bible is not a list of FAQs that your particular problem has to fit within. And the "case" is never closed. Why? Because God doesn't treat us like consumers, clients, or customers. We are His children. We are His friends.

Prayer is more like an ongoing text thread with a close friend. You text when you feel like it. You answer when you want to. You randomly send each other messages, memes, and inside jokes. You talk about what you're planning to do that day and how you're feeling about it. You tell each other what is making you happy, sad, or angry.

There is no pressure or protocol. You just talk.

We need that kind of open communication with God because life is full of complex, unscripted, and often invisible changes. It has unexpected turns and random dark valleys.

When you're in trouble, you don't want heavenly tech support. You don't want a list of FAQs to work through. You don't want a randomly assigned angel to chat with you politely, give you some options, and close the case.

You want to talk with *God*.

Prayer is your link to Him. It's an open line of communication, an ongoing text thread, that is always available to you as you walk through this crazy thing we call life.

Learn to turn to prayer quickly, not as a last resort. Let it be your most familiar tool, your first recourse, your favorite solution.

In other words, keep the conversation going.

3. Growth takes humility.

Early in her career, before becoming a fitness guru and television personality, Jillian Michaels was fired from her job with a talent agency and ended up working as a physical therapy assistant at a gym. It was a slap in the face and a huge pay cut.

It was also the best thing that could have happened to her.

She started from the bottom, but she loved what she was doing, and she was good at it. She gained influence as a trainer, started her own company, was invited to be on *The Biggest Loser*, and has been an influential voice in fitness and television ever since.

Jillian sums up her abrupt career change this way: "A bad day for your ego is a great day for your soul."[2]

I love that. Not when my ego takes a hit—that hurts. But I love the connection she makes between humility and soul success.

Tests and trials and troubles and tribulations are highly effective at taking our egos down a notch. Or two. Or ten. That's a good thing. Why? I'll tell you.

Humility opens us up to change.

Proud people aren't interested in personal growth. Why should they be? They don't need to grow because they have it all together, they think. They see themselves as the teachers, not the students; the experts, not the newbies.

That is, until they hit a problem they can't solve, a situation that brings them back to reality. Then they realize—as we all must from time to time—that none of us have all the answers. We are all learners, and that's okay.

When you hit a difficulty or challenge, quickly admit where you need to grow. Don't pretend to have it all together if you don't. Seek wisdom. Get counsel. Grow in understanding. Ask for advice.

Contrary to popular opinion, _pride_ is the shameful thing, not humility.

This brings us back to prayer. Prayer is an act of humility. When we pray, we recognize that there is a Higher Power. We admit that we don't have it all figured out and we need help.

When we are going through trials and we turn to prayer, we invite both internal and external change. Rather than arrogantly insisting God fix our circumstances, we give Him permission to direct our personal growth.

If prayer isn't changing you, you're not doing it right.

The secret to perfection lies in walking with God in humility.

These three truths—growth takes time, it takes effort, and it takes humility—are not the easiest things to swallow. You might wish growth were quick, easy, and ego-stroking.

Ultimately, though, the process of perfection is one that brings us closer to God. It builds layers of history and intimacy into our relationship with Him. That's why David was a man after God's heart—because year after year, battle after battle, challenge after challenge, even though he made some terrible mistakes along the way, he consistently turned to God. He allowed God to purify and change and challenge and guide him.

You don't have to be perfect overnight. But you do have to allow God to transform you.

If prayer isn't changing you, you're not doing it right.

Get in the car

Prayer and power

When we first moved to LA to start Zoe Church, we were a one-car family. And by that, I mean Julia and the kids had one car, and I had my Uber app.

That was fine at first, but after a few months, I really started turning to God. My prayers usually came from the back seat of those Ubers, partly because some of them drove like they were in a hurry not to get to my destination but to meet Jesus face-to-face right then, and partly because I simply prefer to drive myself. It's more efficient, more comfortable, and more economical.

We couldn't afford another vehicle, so I would tell God, "I need you to buy me a car." Those were my exact words.

I wasn't demanding. I was informing.

Obviously, I wasn't telling God something He didn't already know, but the Bible tells us to ask, seek, and knock. It reminds us that God knows our desires and responds to our petitions. The more I rode in Ubers, the greater my desire grew, and the more frequent those petitions became.

This went on for months, but I didn't give up. I knew we were supposed to have another vehicle, and somehow God was going to make a way.

One day, out of the blue, a friend texted me. He was a pastor in Rancho Cucamonga. He told me his father had just called him and asked him to give me a message: He had been praying that morning, **When we** and the Holy Spirit told him to buy me a car! He said, **pray, we can** "Choose any car you'd like, and we will buy it for you."

expect God Next thing I know, my friend texted me links to two **to respond.** auto agency websites and a ballpark amount to spend. A couple days later, I drove off a lot with a brand-new car.

I will never forget the rush of emotion, gratitude, and awe that flooded through me in that moment. I've always known God answers prayer, and I've seen many answered prayers over the years. But that particular answered prayer stands out in my memory. It was so clearly and dramatically God, and it was far beyond what I could have asked for or expected.

We pray because God responds to our prayers with *power*.

I know we've spent the last few chapters looking at a lot of other things we receive from prayer, including peace, purpose, premise, perspective, presence, process, and perfection.

Those things are, in many ways, more important than receiving what we are praying for specifically. They go deeper and last longer and mean more in the long run. That's why prayer always "works"—because prayer always changes us, even when it doesn't change the circumstance we are praying about.

But—and this is an important *but*—God *also* gives us tangible answers to prayer. We shouldn't emphasize the internal results of prayer at the expense of the external ones. Both are part of prayer, and when we pray, we can expect God to respond.

No, He doesn't owe us anything.

No, He doesn't operate on our timetable.

No, He doesn't give us what we want every time.

No, He doesn't always do things the way we expect.

No, we can't manipulate Him into doing what we want.

But God _does_ answer prayer. He hears the desires of our hearts and responds to our petitions.

He doesn't do it begrudgingly either. Unlike humans, God never gets impatient when we need His help. Instead, He delights in meeting our needs.

POWER THROUGH PRAYER

Getting answers to our prayers is probably the number one reason we pray. There's nothing wrong with that. Prayer is a natural response to need, and it is an expression of our confidence in God. Prayer keeps us humble and connected, and those are always good things.

David wrote in Psalm 34:15, "The eyes of the Lord are on the righteous, and his ears are attentive to their cry." God wants you to express your needs, and He wants you to believe in His goodness and power to help.

Jesus taught on answered prayer many times. Matthew records this particular invitation to pray:

> Ask and it will be given to you; seek and you will find; knock and the door will be opened to you. For everyone who asks receives; the one who seeks finds; and to the one who knocks, the door will be opened.

> Which of you, if your son asks for bread, will give him a stone? Or if he asks for a fish, will give him a snake? If you, then, though you are evil, know how to give good gifts to your children, how much more will your Father in heaven give good gifts to those who ask him!

> 7:7–12

Jesus wasn't encouraging prayer in some meek, half-hearted way or as a last resort. He both taught and modeled a dynamic, interactive prayer life. He prayed all the time, and God moved strongly in response. Just read through the Gospels and note the crazy miracles that followed Jesus everywhere He went.

John, one of Jesus' closest disciples, also knew the power that is found through prayer. He writes this:

> This is the confidence we have in approaching God: that if we ask anything according to his will, he hears us. And if we know that he hears us—whatever we ask—we know that we have what we asked of him.
>
> 1 John 5:14–15

Prayer is more than getting specific answers—but it's not *less* than that. We should celebrate and appreciate all the benefits we've looked at in the last chapters, but we should also pray for specific things. Bold things. Real things. Little things and big things, necessary things and less-than-necessary things, things for us and things for others.

Even though some of our prayers won't be answered in the way we imagined, we will see God's hand at work.

What a crazy thought: Our prayers can move the hand of God!

When God responds to our requests in a tangible way, it is a wonderful, thrilling boost to our faith. It becomes one more proof of God's love for us, yet another testimony in a lifetime of walking with Him.

If you need a faith boost, the Bible contains dozens of specific examples of answered prayer. For example:

Abraham prayed for a son. (Genesis 15)
Hagar prayed for deliverance in the desert. (Genesis 16:7–13)
Moses prayed for help at the Red Sea. (Exodus 14:15–16)

The Israelites prayed for deliverance from Egypt. (Exodus 2:23–25; 3:7–10; Acts 7:34)

Gideon prayed for a sign. (Judges 6:36–40)

Samson prayed for strength. (Judges 16:28–30)

Hannah prayed for a child. (1 Samuel 1:10–17, 19–20)

David prayed for forgiveness and restoration after he sinned. (Psalm 51)

Solomon prayed for wisdom. (1 Kings 3:1–13; 9:2–3)

Elijah prayed for a widow's son to come back to life. (1 Kings 17:22)

Jabez prayed for prosperity. (1 Chronicles 4:10)

The priests and Levites prayed blessing over the people. (2 Chronicles 30:27)

Daniel prayed for the interpretation of Nebuchadnezzar's dream. (Daniel 2:19–23)

A leper prayed for healing. (Matthew 8:2–3; Mark 1:40–43; Luke 5:12–13)

A centurion prayed for his servant. (Matthew 8:5–13; Luke 7:3–10; John 4:50–51)

Peter prayed for Tabitha to be brought back to life. (Acts 9:40)

The disciples prayed for Peter's deliverance from prison. (Acts 12:5–17)

These are just a handful of the times God answered the prayers of an individual or group of people. There are many more, plus countless promises and invitations to take our needs before the Lord in prayer.

PRAYER IS A VEHICLE

Prayer, as I said in the first chapter, is the vehicle, not the destination. Prayer's power is found in its ability to carry us into God's intimate presence, to open our hearts to His, and to bring heaven to earth.

Do you remember your first car? I remember mine. I got it when I was sixteen years old. It was a puke-green-colored 1978 Plymouth Volare. The thing was an absolute clunker. I nicknamed it The Hoopty. While she wasn't much to look at, she got me to school and basketball practice and back, and that was all that mattered.

Really, though, the point of a car is not to look pretty. I mean, we'd all prefer a Lambo over a jalopy, but what matters most is that the thing gets us from Point A to Point B. A good paint job, leather interior, and Bluetooth connectivity are a plus, but four tires and a functioning motor are the important things.

In the same way, the point of prayer is not to look good or sound good—it's to get us somewhere. True prayer doesn't focus on flashiness, but on effectiveness. On power. On getting us from Point A (our current situation) to Point B (the presence of God).

Our faith is more than just ritual or even morality; it's a relationship with a living God. A real being who sees, hears, thinks, feels, and acts.

That is why prayer is not about memorizing magic formulas or incantations. It's not about how loud we pray or how eloquent we are. It's not about us at all.

Prayer is about God.

We pray to God, we pray according to His will, we pray for His involvement, and we pray in Jesus' name. Prayer starts, continues, and ends with God. It finds its power in Him. Prayer carries us to the throne room of heaven, to the very source of infinite creativity and grace and power.

Prayer is not powerful. God is.

God is the reason we pray. Prayer in and of itself has no power. It's just words. But the words are directed to God, and they move the heart of God. He responds to our needs and to our expression of those needs.

When we pray, we need to realize that we are tapping in to the resources of heaven. That is no small thing. When the Bible encourages us to pray in faith, it's talking about praying from an expansive, awestruck awareness of the nature of God. He wants us to focus on how big He is, not on how big our problems are.

We might be small, but we can pray big prayers.

We might be weak, but we can trust in God's strength.

We might be uncertain, but we can be sure of His love.

We might be tempted, but we can find a way out through Jesus.

We might be sinful, but we are forgiven and accepted by grace.

We might be anxious, but we find our peace in His presence.

We might be grieving, but we can rejoice that God will carry us through.

Our prayers must be bathed in the certainty that God hears us and that He is able to help. We know God is there. We know He cares. We know He intervenes in human existence. And so, we pray, and God acts.

Get in the car, friend.

FRIENDS OF JESUS

Prayer might seem like an unnecessary activity when you think about God's omniscience. Why pray if God already knows what you're going to ask? Why pray if He has a better plan than you could ever come up with? Why pray if what you're asking for might just mess things up even more?

We've probably all wondered these things at one point or another. I don't have it all figured out. I think the interplay between God's sovereignty and our humanity will always have an element of mystery to it.

I do know, though, that when we pray, we partner with God. We participate in His sovereign rule. I think that's part of what Jesus meant when He told us to pray, "Your kingdom come, your will be done, on earth as it is in heaven"

(Matthew 6:10). Our prayers and our efforts are aligned with His will, and together we are bringing heaven to earth.

Toward the end of His life on earth, Jesus told His disciples this:

> You are my friends if you do what I command. I no longer call you servants, because a servant does not know his master's business. Instead, I have called you friends, for everything that I learned from my Father I have made known to you. You did not choose me, but I chose you and appointed you so that you might go and bear fruit—fruit that will last—and so that whatever you ask in my name the Father will give you. This is my command: Love each other.
>
> John 15:14–17

Notice the key words here: *friends, fruit, ask, love.*

First, Jesus was saying that they were all friends. The disciples weren't just servants, they were friends. There was trust and open communication between them. This same relationship continues with us today. We are friends of God.

Second, this friendship was going to result in teamwork. "Fruit" refers to work. The disciples (again, that includes us) would bear fruit. What we do is in Jesus' name and in alignment with God's will, and it will have positive results.

Third, prayer was going to be a key element of this relationship. Jesus refers to "whatever [they] ask," which implies they were going to be doing a great deal of asking, talking, listening, and learning in prayer.

Fourth, they would love one another. Earlier He had said they would also remain in His love (verse 9). We are connected to God and each other through love, teamwork, and open communication.

What does this mean for us? It means that our prayers help bring to pass God's will on the earth. In a very real sense, when we pray, we are working together with God.

Yes, in His sovereignty He knows what we are going to pray. But He still invites us to participate. Crazy as it seems, He takes our prayers into account, and He chooses to let them influence Him.

That's what friends do, after all. They dream together, they love each other, and they share a common purpose.

Our role as partners or participants in God's work is not based on our own merit, of course. That's why Jesus was insistent earlier in John 15 that we abide in Him just as He abides in God (verses 1–10). That means abiding in both His love and His commands.

Our prayers help bring to pass God's will on the earth. In a very real sense, when we pray, we are working together with God.

When we pray "in Jesus' name," we are reminding ourselves that the basis for our prayers is Jesus, not us. We aren't coming before His throne claiming we deserve to be heard or that God owes us anything. But we aren't groveling in fear either, terrified that He'll see our weaknesses and failures and ignore our needs as a result. Our prayers are grounded not in how we perform but in who we are: friends of Jesus.

The basis of our prayer, the authority of our prayer, the power of our prayer—it comes from Jesus.

Just as Jesus walked this earth doing what the Father did and saying what the Father said (John 5:19; 14:24), so we pray and act according to God's will. That doesn't mean we are robots or puppets, blindly following the will of God. He gives us a great amount of free will—more than we probably realize at times. He does not dominate or subjugate us; rather, He brings us into an interdependent relationship with Him.

Sometimes He asks our opinion.

Sometimes He lets us take the lead.

Sometimes His decision is influenced by our desires.

Sometimes He waits for us to ask before He decides to act.

Sometimes He gives us options, then guides us into blessing regardless of what we choose.

It would be arrogant—and impossible—for me to try to break down what this partnership looks like in every circumstance and for every person. I can't always figure it out for my own life, much less for yours!

All I know is that when I pray, God involves me in His work. And when I want to do His will, I find myself praying.

God's will and our prayers are intricately and inseparably connected. It's the whole chicken-and-egg dynamic: Who can tell where God's work stops and ours starts, or where ours ends and His begins?

Did my prayers move God to replace those death-wish Uber rides with a brand-new car? Or did God move my heart to pray for what He already planned to give me?

Yes.

That's all I can say because that's all I know. And I'm okay with that.

We pray and God acts. He leads and we follow. We ask and He gives. He loves us and we love Him back.

There is power in that partnership that goes far beyond what we've realized. And that is the beautiful thing about prayer.

It always invites us into more of God.

We've spent the last few chapters exploring some of the many ways prayer benefits us. There are more, I'm sure. And we've barely scratched the surface on the ones we have covered.

It's enough to get started, though. After all, prayer is one of those things you will only fully understand once you start doing it.

It's kind of like wakeboarding. I could tell you how wakeboarding feels. I could try to explain the physics behind it. I could even show you videos of someone doing it. But you still won't really know what wakeboarding is.

You have to do it.

You have to actually feel the sudden rush of water propel your board and your body out of the water and onto the surface. You have to discover the freedom of skipping across the waves under a power that is not your own. You have to get a feel for the way your shifting weight moves you across the wake, into the air, and back down.

There is only one way to learn to wakeboard, and there is only one way to learn to pray: You have to do it. As you do, you'll experience for yourself the myriad results of prayer.

Pray your way to peace.
Pray your way to purpose.
Pray your way to premise.
Pray your way to perspective.
Pray your way to presence.
Pray your way to process.
Pray your way to perfection.
Pray your way to power.

WHAT EVERYBODY GETS WRONG ABOUT PRAYER

When it comes to exercising regularly, there are two kinds of people: those who find something that works for them and do it for the next four decades, and those who try new things every four months.

Both are awesome, in my opinion. Just do what works for you. Period.

If you're bored and want to do something different, go for it. Try mountain climbing. Or slacklining. Or fencing. Or synchronized swimming. Or whatever gets you and keeps you moving. If you'd rather do the same thing for forty years, that's fine too. It will cost you less in exercise paraphernalia and closet space than changing it up multiple times a year, that's for sure.

The best exercise routine is the one you'll actually follow. *Not* exercising is the real problem.

The thing is, if you aren't exercising, it's not as easy as "just starting." Anyone who has struggled to start a regular workout program has had to deal with the underlying reasons why they don't exercise.

Prayer works the same way. There are lots of ways to pray, e.g., routines and methods. We'll look at some of them in the last section of this book. But before we address those, we need to look at some things that could undermine your prayer life before you even get going. These are things that, like bad habits in exercise, could actually hurt you if they aren't adjusted.

We'll look at reasons you might not be praying, prayers that are a waste of time, prayers that give up too easily, using prayers as excuses, dealing with unanswered prayer, and more.

It takes honesty to confront the things holding you back. But as my Peloton instructor, Jess Sims, always says, "No ego, amigo!"

Whether you prefer to change up your prayer routine all the time or find something that works for you for decades to come, that's up to you. But don't *not* pray. That would be the only failure.

TEN

How to dodge ducks

There are few forces on earth that can make California drivers slow down, much less stop en masse. So if you're driving down the freeway and suddenly see a wall of brake lights in the distance, you know there is a real problem.

It's probably either a) road construction, b) a wreck, or c) a mother duck and her ducklings crossing the road.

That last one really happens, by the way. Ducks with death wishes occasionally try to cross I-5, the main interstate on the West Coast, triggering traffic jams and news reports. Why are they crossing the road? Nobody knows. (Except the chicken, possibly, and he's not talking.)

There is something inherently frustrating about traffic jams, regardless of what causes them. And I don't think I'm the only one to feel this, but as you are inching along, surrounded by hundreds or thousands of other frustrated motorists, you start to question the existence of humanity. Or at least the competency of the civil engineers responsible for the roads.

Traffic is meant to *flow*. Vehicles are designed to *move*.

Here's my point: If traffic isn't moving on the freeway, something is blocking it. And until that thing is taken care of, we're going to be stuck in a traffic jam, listening to podcasts (if I'm alone) or the Kidz Bop playlist (if I'm with the family), while time ticks by.

In the same way, prayers were meant to flow, to move, to go somewhere. So if our prayer life is not flowing, something is probably blocking it. But instead of roadwork or ducks, that something is usually internal, subtle, easy to miss.

Prayer comes naturally to humans. The practice of praying is present in religions the world over. Prayer is simply talking, after all. Humans learn to talk early in life and then never really shut up. It only makes sense we would talk to God too.

Since prayer is natural, if we aren't praying regularly, there is usually a reason. If we want to pray more, we need to figure out what is getting in the way. Often, though, we don't take the time to figure out what the obstacle is. We just feel guilty for not praying more.

Why do we feel guilty? Because we know we should pray more. We've heard about prayer, read about prayer, maybe even tried prayer. We might even really like praying. But we just don't do it as often as we wish we would or know we should.

We find ourselves praying when we need something, of course. But then we feel guilty about only talking to God when we have a request. Like the rich uncle you never think about until you need someone to cosign on an apartment lease.

The good news is that God does not shame us for our lack of prayer. Why would He? Prayer is for us, not for Him. If we don't pray, God isn't the one missing out. I think He misses us, of course, but it's not like our lack of prayer can take anything away from an infinite God.

So if you aren't praying as much as you'd like to, remember that God is not mad at you, and you don't need to shame yourself.

Finding and eliminating obstacles to prayer is not about shame. When you ask yourself why you aren't praying more, the goal is not to beat yourself over the head with a Bible, obsess over all the things you're doing wrong, or tell yourself that you don't measure up.

The goal is to grow in understanding.

Shame won't fix anything. It is the absolute worst motivator. Shame promises to help you change, and for a brief period it seems like it's working. The self-imposed punishment almost feels good, in a masochistic way, like you're paying for your sins or something. It motivates you to do some things differently to avoid the shame.

Ask yourself honestly: What obstacles could be getting in the way of a healthy prayer life?

But ultimately shame only discourages you more.

Why? Because as soon as you start to improve, the shame subsides—and with it, your motivation to keep going. So you fall back into old habits. And shame comes back around. And you change again, temporarily, just until you silence shame's voice. And so on, and so forth, ad infinitum, ad nauseam.

My friend, get off the shame train. It's not taking you where you want to go.

Instead, ask yourself honestly: What obstacles could be getting in the way of a healthy prayer life? Let's look at a few possibilities.

1. IGNORANCE: I DON'T UNDERSTAND IT.

It's hard to do things you don't understand. Calculus, for example. Or braiding hair. Maybe one or both of those are easy for you, but they're not for me. So I avoid them both.

If you can't figure out how to do something, you either learn, or you tend to avoid it. It's human nature.

Prayer is not hard, but it does have a bit of a learning curve because it's a spiritual act, and some of us might not be used to engaging the spiritual side of our being. If you think back to when you learned to ride a bike or swim or read, though, you might remember how impossible that activity seemed—until you crossed a certain invisible threshold, and suddenly it started to click.

Honestly, that's the whole point behind this book. I want to demystify prayer. I want it to feel second-nature to you, like riding a bike or reading a book. That doesn't happen overnight, but it also doesn't take a lifetime.

Don't be intimidated by prayer. Don't overcomplicate it. Don't hide from it. Prayer is not some esoteric mystery that only a hyper-spiritual few can master. It isn't reserved for pastors and preachers and saints.

Prayer is for everyone, and everyone can pray.

You can do this.

2. INEXPERIENCE: I'M NOT GOOD AT IT.

It's one thing to gain information and understanding, but it's another to have actual experience.

Have you ever been at a party and innocently asked someone what they liked to do for fun, and they launched into a thirty-minute monologue about surfing or snowboarding or stargazing or something else you have no idea how to do? They were clearly passionate about it, and they talked until your eyes glazed over a bit.

You probably learned more than you ever wanted to about their hobby, but that doesn't mean you could do what they do. You had head knowledge (and maybe a headache), but you didn't have any firsthand experience. So you really had no idea how to do it.

There is a reason job interviews tend to focus more on real-life experience than just about any other qualification. There is simply no substitute for hands-on proficiency.

Prayer is the same. You can read this book and five others from cover to cover, but if you don't actually pray, you'll never know "how" to pray. To get good at prayer, you have to do it.

We taught our kids to make their own beds starting when they were about three years old. When they would first try, their reply was always the same: "Dad, I can't, I'm not very good at it."

You can guess how I replied. "You can; you just need practice!"

That never went over well. But it was true. Now they are bed-making pros, and someday their spouses are going to thank us for that.

The same principle is true in prayer. Not being good at something doesn't mean you *can't* be good at it. It just means you need practice.

If you've ever felt a little intimidated by prayer or unsure what to say, don't give up. Instead, lean in. Experiment. Learn what works for you, what you like the best, how prayer fits in with your unique personality and your current schedule.

There really aren't any rules or protocols for how you have to pray. There are some things you should avoid (as we'll see in the next chapter), but for the most part, prayer will come naturally, and it will get easier the more you do it.

What do you have to lose? Nothing but worry, feeling overwhelmed, hurts and wounds, and a lot of other things you'd rather not be carrying.

3. BOREDOM: I DON'T LIKE DOING IT.

In general, we avoid boring activities, and we gravitate toward rewarding ones.

That doesn't mean we never do things that bore us—we do them all the time. We have to. Work, study, paying bills, mowing the lawn, and a thousand more things fill our time. We might wish we could avoid them, but we're adults, so we don't. Or we do, then we wish we hadn't.

Prayer should not be one of the things that we "have" to do. If it is, we'll tend to avoid it. We'll put it off. We'll pray only when absolutely necessary.

Many people see prayer as boring because they've been taught that we do it in order to receive some intangible, undefined benefit from God. It's seen as a spiritual discipline that somehow helps us. Just do it, we're told, whether you feel like it or not.

I am firmly opposed to that approach to prayer.

Now, we'll talk in a moment about being disciplined and intentional about prayer. I understand the importance of pushing through the initial resistance your body and mind might have to prayer. Sometimes you do pray because you know you should, even when you don't feel like it.

When you realize the power of prayer, it goes from being boring to rewarding, from being a "have to" to a "love to."

But that doesn't mean we have to force ourselves to pray all the time.

Hopefully the benefits we covered in the first section helped excite you about prayer. Prayer produces results that are both internal and external, short-term and long-term, individual and corporate, mental and spiritual. Prayer changes you from the moment you start doing it and it continues to work long after you've stopped.

When you realize the power of prayer, it goes from being boring to rewarding, from being a "have to" to a "love to."

4. DISCOURAGEMENT: IT DOESN'T WORK.

Have you ever weighed yourself after a workout and been frustrated that you didn't shed any pounds after such intense exercise? Maybe you even went *up* half a pound because you guzzled a bottle of water.

Mentally, you know it doesn't work that way. Exercise isn't just about burning calories in the moment. It's about increasing your metabolism and overall health so that your body burns calories all day long. Plus, losing weight isn't the only goal. You want your body to be healthy, not fit into some stereotype that society has created. You want to build muscle, stay flexible, and have good circulation.

In other words, exercise accomplishes more than what you see reflected on the scale or in your mirror. It keeps working for you all day long, not just in the moment. And its benefits go beyond just weight loss.

In the same way, prayer works for you long after you're done praying, and its benefits go beyond simply answered prayer. We looked at that in detail in section 1.

And yet, many of us are so focused on getting quick, visible answers to prayer that we give up when they don't happen. That's like stopping your workouts because the scale didn't change four minutes after you ran a 5K.

Prayer is always working for you, day and night, in a hundred different ways. Give it time, and understand what results you're looking for. Have a wholistic, long-term approach to prayer and you'll be a lot more motivated.

5. SHAME: I'M EMBARRASSED.

Remember the dentist example earlier? We avoid people who shame us.

If we find ourselves avoiding God, sometimes it can be because we are ashamed of who we are or how we've failed. Maybe we think God is judging us, so we subconsciously stay away from Him.

That sense of failure and condemnation is a greater enemy than you might realize. It will hold you back not just from prayer, but from faith, from serving, from taking risks.

Here's a suggestion: Don't avoid prayer because of shame; use prayer to *fight* shame. If you feel embarrassed or insecure before God, take time to pray through some Bible verses that affirm your standing before Him.

In prayer, you can reprogram the way you think.

Changing the way you think will change the way you feel.

Changing the way you think and feel will change the way you act.

And that will change your life.

Need some suggestions of Bible verses that will help you fight shame? Here are a handful, but there are many more.

- "For God did not send his Son into the world to condemn the world, but to save the world through him. Whoever believes in him is not condemned." (John 3:17–18)
- "Therefore, there is now no condemnation for those who are in Christ Jesus." (Romans 8:1)
- "Therefore, since we have been justified through faith, we have peace with God through our Lord Jesus Christ, through whom we have gained access by faith into this grace in which we now stand." (Romans 5:1–2)
- "Neither height nor depth, nor anything else in all creation, will be able to separate us from the love of God that is in Christ Jesus our Lord." (Romans 8:39)
- "Therefore, if anyone is in Christ, the new creation has come: The old has gone, the new is here!" (2 Corinthians 5:17)
- "If our hearts condemn us, we know that God is greater than our hearts, and he knows everything. Dear friends, if our hearts do not condemn us, we have confidence before God." (1 John 3:20–21).

6. FLESH: I DON'T WANT TO DO IT.

Let's be honest. Sometimes we don't pray because we don't feel like it. There are other things that seem more fun or exciting in the moment, like scrolling Instagram or reorganizing the furniture or making a fourth cup of coffee.

In other words, sometimes our momentary desires fight against our long-term goals.

The apostle Paul wrote, "I do not understand what I do. For what I want to do I do not do, but what I hate I do" (Romans 7:15). I find that verse strangely comforting. If Paul couldn't keep his desires under control all the time, then maybe my struggles are more normal than that voice of shame would like me to think.

The Bible uses the word *flesh* to describe the self-centered, destructive desires within us that lead us into making dumb decisions. It's like that little cartoon devil sitting on your shoulder talking you into doing something you'll regret.

The fact that our flesh and spirits struggle with each other doesn't mean we are bad people or that the desires we feel are inherently wrong. Many of them—such as the desires for food, pleasure, sex, rest, friends, importance, peace, and safety—are an important part of being human.

We've probably all realized, though, that what we *want* to do is often not what we *should* do.

We *want* to binge a Netflix series until two in the morning, but we know we have to be at school at eight, so we force ourselves to go to bed earlier.

We *want* to quit our job and learn to surf, but we instead we work Monday to Friday and postpone surfing until the weekend.

We *want* to yell at our neighbors because their dog won't stop barking, but instead we turn on a fan and sleep with headphones and music.

Wants and desires are like an appetite for food. Appetites can be developed. They can be changed. If you stop eating a particular thing, such as dairy or meat, you can lose your appetite for it after a while. On the other hand, if you regularly eat something you don't love, such as salad or vegetables, you eventually develop an appetite for it.

The same goes for the desires that war inside our minds, wills, and emotions. Not only can we lose the appetite for egging houses, we can develop an appetite for things like prayer, reading the Bible, loving people, being generous, smiling more (what a thought!), and so on.

The more you pray, the more you want to pray, and the greater your appetite for the things of the spirit becomes.

7. DISORGANIZATION: I DON'T HAVE TIME TO DO IT.

I think one of the biggest obstacles to prayer is lack of organization. We don't do what we don't schedule.

James Clear wrote in his book *Atomic Habits*, "You do not rise to the level of your goals. You fall to the level of your systems."[1]

There are a lot of things I want to do that I have to *plan* to do or they'll never happen. Dating my wife is one of them. Julia and I love to go out together. Date nights are our happy place. But if we don't put some serious planning and work into organizing those nights out, they'll never happen.

Similarly, we need to plan for prayer. Planning doesn't diminish the beauty or authenticity of prayer any more than scheduling a date removes its romance. If anything, planning ahead makes our prayer life (and our dating life) more special. It gives us something to look forward to.

I'm not going to tell you when to pray or how long to pray. That's up to you.

Your prayer times will change over the course of your life. There will be seasons you just have to squeeze in moments of prayer between the craziness of day-to-day schedules, and there will be times when you have long, uninterrupted talks with God.

That's okay.

Don't frustrate yourself by trying to meet some artificial, subjective, legalistic ideal of what your prayer life should look like.

In case you're curious, here is what my prayer schedule looks like now. It could change without warning, but this arrangement is working for me pretty well.

1. I read my Bible every morning, then I spend a few minutes—maybe five or so—praying. I usually write out my prayers, but that's just me.

2. I pray quick prayers throughout the day as needed: for a need, for a person, for a problem, for strength. These are lightning prayers that last a few seconds and often are not spoken out loud.

3. I pray nightly with my boys when they go to bed. I pray specifically for them: what I feel for them, what they are going through, what they are concerned about.

4. We have a weekly prayer meeting at our church on Saturdays at 6:00 p.m. that I usually lead or attend.

5. Every Sunday I pray throughout the morning, and we also spend a few minutes praying with the volunteer team for the services.

6. During our Sunday services, right after worship, we pray together as a church for needs people have.

As you can see from the above list, for me, prayer is not about quantity. These are not long prayer times, for the most part. I don't time my prayers. I pray frequently, though.

I pray about everything, so I'm anxious about nothing. That's not just a book title. It's the way I live.

Remember, I have a full-time job, four children, and a couple of hobbies, so it's not like I sit around all day with nothing to do. On the other hand, my full-time job includes prayer, so I get paid to pray, in a sense. Those things are unique to me.

So please *don't* compare yourself to me. You don't have my life, and I don't have yours. I'm not your example of prayer.

Jesus is.

You can always find someone "worse" at prayer (whatever that means) if you want to feel superior, but you can also find someone "better" if you want to feel discouraged. But that all seems a little pointless, doesn't it?

Just get started. Pray a little, then pray a little more.

How about if we stop looking at everyone else, and instead we pray however and whenever we can? How about if we develop a personal relationship with God and let that relationship grow and shift organically, rather than trying to impress anyone else?

I need prayer, and you do too! We need more prayer, not less prayer.

Just get started. Pray a little, then pray a little more. Don't let ignorance, inexperience, boredom, discouragement, shame, flesh, disorganization, or even a line of adorable ducks block your prayers.

Go around the obstacles. Dodge the ducks.

Once you experience the peace and the power of prayer, you'll never stop.

ELEVEN

These prayers are a waste of time

Julia and I have moved to a new city or a new house several times in our marriage. That is a test of both mental and marital strength, if we're being honest here. There's one thing in particular that amazes me every time we move: how much junk we've managed to collect.

We're not hoarders. We're the opposite of hoarders, whatever that is. Anti-hoarders? Clutter-haters? Enemies of all the things? I don't know.

My point is, we consider ourselves relatively neat, orderly, and efficient, yet we still have massive amounts of useless things crammed into cupboards and corners and cubbyholes, all because we "might need that someday."

Single socks, for example. We have an entire collection of them. Why are we stockpiling single socks? Do we really have faith that their partners are going to return for them? Do we expect to someday lose a leg? It's probably not going to happen. They are useless socks.

Ironically, one of our greatest sources of clutter is storage containers. That's right—storage *solutions* are actually creating storage *problems* in the Veach household. Julia loves Netflix shows about tidying up, so she'll get inspired to organize things in a new and better way. That naturally means purchasing more bins. The Holy Laws of Decluttering state that bins have to match each other, though, so she buys multiple bins at once. But since the old bins still hold some emotional promise of helping reduce clutter, she doesn't throw those out. So we now have approximately five thousand plastic bins of assorted sizes, shapes, and colors. An empty storage bin is a double curse: It takes up lots of space without reducing any clutter. It's as useless as a single sock, and it's a lot bigger.

I could go on, of course. Not just about the forgotten junk stacked in the nooks and crannies of our homes, but about the other useless things we spend our time and money on. Sometimes we look back and wonder, *Why did I waste so much of myself on that activity, that belief, that offense, that business, that addiction, that investment, that mistake?*

Nobody should live in regret, so the only reason to look backward is to look forward. That is, we learn from the past to improve our future. This goes for prayer too.

Not all prayer is good prayer. There are some ways of praying that are just as useless as single socks and empty storage bins.

Maybe you've prayed these kinds of prayers. I know I have. If we're going to be effective in our prayer lives, we need to identify the prayers that are wasting our time and God's time. (Can you even waste an eternal being's time? I have no idea.) Once we identify them, we can replace useless prayers with prayers that matter.

1. HYPOCRITICAL PRAYER

The word *hypocrite* comes from the Greek word for actor. It could also have a negative meaning, referring to someone who was playing a part to deceive others. German theologian Gerhard Kittel wrote, "The stage is a sham world and actors are deceivers. Hence *hypókrisis* takes on the sense of 'pretense' or 'pretext.'"[1]

Hypocritical prayer is all for show. It's a drama, a performance, a sham. Jesus addressed hypocrites very bluntly, as only He could:

> And when you pray, do not be like the hypocrites, for they love to pray standing in the synagogues and on the street corners to be seen by others. Truly I tell you, they have received their reward in full. But when you pray, go into your room, close the door and pray to your Father, who is unseen. Then your Father, who sees what is done in secret, will reward you.
>
> Matthew 6:5–6

Jesus seems to have had specific people in mind when He called out the "hypocrites" among them. Maybe some of them were listening to Him right then. They were likely the religious leaders of the day who tended to make a big show of their spirituality.

Jesus says they loved to pray "standing in the synagogues and on street corners." Synagogues were religious centers, and the street corners were business and social centers. In other words, wherever they went, they showed off how spiritual they were.

The problem wasn't that people heard them pray. Public, corporate prayer is seen throughout the Bible. The problem was that they prayed specifically "to be seen by others" (verse 5). That was their goal. Performance was the point.

Jesus says that they received the payment they wanted: applause. Their reputation went up. People saw them as super spiritual. Parents pointed them out to their children as examples of holiness. "Normal" people felt intimidated, even guilty, when they heard them pray.

The hypocrites wanted praise, and they got it. That was all they got, though.

Because God wasn't even listening.

They weren't talking to Him, so why should He care what they said? They were praying for people to hear, which isn't prayer at all. It's simply talking into the air.

In prayer, as in everything else, our hearts matter most to God.

In prayer, as in everything else, our hearts matter most to God. He isn't impressed with showy acts, with clever words, with rituals or rites or performances. God sees our inner selves. He knows our motivations better than we do.

God loves the kind of prayer that is birthed out of genuine relationship, not out of pride. The poet Mary Oliver writes that prayer is not a competition, but rather a doorway into gratitude and silence.[2] It leads to a conversation with a God who responds when we approach Him in humility.

That is the reward we should be seeking: not the praise of people, but the presence of God.

2. BABBLING PRAYERS

After Jesus finished roasting hypocrites and their performative prayers, He took aim at another wrong form of prayer: empty, repetitive babblings.

> And when you pray, do not keep on babbling like pagans, for they think they will be heard because of their many words. Do not be like them, for your Father knows what you need before you ask him.
>
> Matthew 6:7–8

I love the word *babbling*. It is onomatopoeia, meaning the word itself sounds like what it means.

Babble. Babababababble. Meaningless syllables strung together.

It is thought that the Greek word here is also onomatopoeic: *battalogeo* means to stammer, chatter, or babble on.[3] It comes from a root word which—similar to the English word—sounds like baby noises.

Imagine someone blah-blah-blahing long after you've tuned them out. That's what Jesus is talking about here: people who pray long, flowery, wordy prayers with zero content. Their prayers are mere words, empty nonsense designed to impress or manipulate, not to communicate.

Even God is bored by those prayers.

Jesus says that pagans pray with this mindset, thinking that "they will be heard because of their many words" (verse 7). He would have been thinking of people outside the Jewish religion. Rather than believing in one God who loved His people and heard their prayers, they often believed in a pantheon of gods who could be convinced, manipulated, and even played against one another.

Sometimes we pray that same way, though. We believe in one God, but we can still fall into the trap of thinking we can convince or manipulate Him into doing what we want. If we say enough things, if we use the right phrases, if we pay the price by praying enough, God will act on our behalf.

As a parent, I know exactly when my kids are trying to do this to me. They aren't doing it from an evil heart, and neither are we when we pray this way to God. I don't respond well to it from my kids, though. First, because they don't need to convince me to be good to them. That comes naturally to me. Second, because I find it slightly insulting that they think they can manipulate me into doing something (or that they need to).

But again, we do this to God in prayer sometimes. Or we try to, anyway. We think—subconsciously, more than likely—that we can persuade God to do what we want if we can just get the wording right or repeat ourselves often enough. He sees through that even more quickly than parents do.

We don't need to use a lot of words in our prayers. That's the point of the Lord's Prayer, which Jesus taught in the verses following this comment about babbling prayers. He was showing that content and sincerity are what matter, not word count.

3. BITTER PRAYERS

In Matthew 6, Jesus taught about hypocritical prayers and babbling prayers, then He gave the Lord's Prayer, which we'll look at in a later chapter. Then, on the heels of all that, He said:

> For if you forgive other people when they sin against you, your heavenly Father will also forgive you. But if you do not forgive others their sins, your Father will not forgive your sins.
>
> Matthew 6:14–15

Those are strong words. Essentially, He's saying we shouldn't go to God in prayer and ask Him to grant us what we won't grant others: grace, mercy, compassion, understanding, forgiveness.

Jesus says the same thing in Matthew 18:21–35, in a parable about a servant who was forgiven an enormous debt by his master, then went to a fellow servant and tried to collect a miniscule debt by force.

The Lord's Prayer itself contains the line, "Forgive us our debts, as we also have forgiven our debtors" (Matthew 6:12). Forgiveness is something we give and receive.

If we are harboring offense and bitterness against someone else, God wants us to take care of it, not pretend like everything is fine. One chapter earlier, we read this teaching by Jesus:

> Therefore, if you are offering your gift at the altar and there remember that your brother or sister has something against you, leave your gift there in front of the altar. First go and be reconciled to them; then come and offer your gift.
>
> Matthew 5:23–24

Forgiveness is a big topic, beyond the scope of this section, but I want to emphasize that forgiveness does *not* mean:

- that you no longer feel pain or loss
- that you don't seek justice
- that you don't make sure you are safe from further harm
- that you let the aggressor back into your life or give them control
- that are there are no consequences for what they did

Far too often, the "please forgive me, I'll never do it again" line is used as a control tactic by chronic abusers. They demand forgiveness, not because they are repentant, but because they want to avoid consequences or continue their abuse.

I don't believe Jesus was talking about that at all here when He commanded forgiveness. These chapters do not address oppression or harm perpetrated by people in power, but rather peer-level forgiveness. (Matthew 5:23 says that "your brother or sister" has something against you, for example.)

There is always a place for calling out abuse, drawing limits, and demanding justice. This is especially true when the abuse and injustice is systemic, meaning that it is built into a system and tends to harm the same people over and over.

God help us, in every arena and sphere, to listen to the voices of those who are hurt by systems we have built or societies that benefit us more than them. We are in this together, and we need each other.

In a sense, this mutuality is the point of forgiveness among peers. We are all children of God, which means we are brothers and sisters. We all need forgiveness. We all need reconciliation. We all need to release the bitterness and offense that so easily block the heart-flow of love.

As Katherine Schwarzenegger writes in her book *The Gift of Forgiveness*, "Forgiveness done right is a gift, and, done well, it can work miracles."[4]

Again, the dynamics involved in abuse are a much larger topic, particularly if what you are experiencing has created genuine trauma. The last thing I want to do is threaten you with hellfire and brimstone just because you can't "get over it" faster! And I firmly believe Jesus feels the same way. These passages are not insisting that you gloss over things in some superficial, dismissive, gaslighting way, but rather that you face them with honesty and courage.

Many times, though, our pain isn't due to deep trauma or long-term abuse, but to mistakes someone made, or betrayal, or miscommunication, or unfulfilled expectations, or some other human flaw.

If we become collectors of offenses, two things will happen. First, our world will get smaller and smaller because we will keep kicking people out of it; and second, our prayers will be hindered because our hearts will be too full of hurt to let love in.

If you can't pray because you're so mad at someone, pray for the person you're mad at. Pray through your pain. Pray until you begin to get clarity about how to find healing, even if it's only the next step in the process.

Forgiveness is for you, mostly. It keeps you from being controlled by another person or by your past. It keeps you from breaking your stride.

Prayer can both awaken memories and heal trauma. It's not always easy, and it's not always quick, but praying through your hurts and offenses can bring deep healing to your soul.

If necessary, reach out to someone—a pastor, trained counselor, or trusted mentor—who can walk with you through this and advise you on what steps to take. Prayer is not a substitute for processing trauma or taking practical action, but it is an invaluable aid as you walk the path of healing.

4. COMPLACENT PRAYERS

I remember a young man in our church who was always available to volunteer, run errands, or pick me up at the airport. I appreciated his willingness to help out, but eventually I started to wonder how he had so much free time.

The next time he was driving me somewhere, I casually asked him if he had a job.

"No," he replied. "I'm praying for one, though. God's going to give me a miracle job."

"So how do you pay your bills?" I asked.

"Well, you know, I'm living by faith. Sometimes people Venmo money to me and stuff like that."

We sometimes use praying to avoid doing.

We talked a bit more. I could see that he was a great guy with a lot to offer, but he wasn't taking much initiative.

Finally, I said, "Bro, you can't keep going this way. You know how a miracle job shows up? You apply for ten jobs. God will bless you—but give Him something to work with here."

To his credit, that's exactly what he did. Volunteering at church is great—but I'd much rather see this young man fulfilling his God-given potential than avoiding it.

When it comes to prayer, we sometimes use *praying* to avoid *doing*. Like that young man, we have a lot to offer. But for one reason or another—maybe laziness, maybe fear, maybe some misguided idea of sovereignty—we hold back. We wait for God to make the first move.

What if God is waiting on you to make the first move?

If you're going to pray, be willing to work. Don't pray from a place of complacency, but from one of expectancy. Pray with a mindset of initiative, creativity, and self-confidence. Give God something to work with.

When it comes to members of my staff, I nearly always prefer *doing* over *waiting*. I'd rather tell someone to slow down than to speed up, and I'd rather work with someone who has bad ideas than no ideas.

I think God is the same way with us. Yes, we pray about everything. But that doesn't mean we lie down and take a nap until He zaps us with a lightning bolt to get us moving. Unless we hear otherwise, we need to move forward, trusting in God's calling and His gifts in us, and listening for His direction as we advance.

If you expect God to direct your path, start walking. He can't lead you if you're not moving.

5. NARCISSISTIC PRAYERS

The quintessentially practical apostle James had this to say about prayer:

> What causes fights and quarrels among you? Don't they come from your desires that battle within you? You desire but do not have, so you kill. You covet but you cannot get what you want, so you quarrel and fight. You do not have because you do not ask God. When you ask, you do not receive, because you ask with wrong motives, that you may spend what you get on your pleasures.
>
> 4:1–3

James is not criticizing *what* they are asking for, but rather *why* they are asking for it: to spend what they get on their pleasures.

He's calling them selfish, essentially. And he wants them to know that God doesn't respond to selfish prayers.

James first points out how much fighting there was among them. Then he connects their unanswered prayers to their quarrels by emphasizing the root cause of both: they only cared about getting, taking, grabbing, hoarding. It was textbook narcissism.

He's talking to us too, of course. If our approach to either community or prayer is primarily self-focused, we miss the point. And eventually we'll mess them both up.

We don't exist in a bubble, and we don't pray in a bubble. We're not islands unto ourselves. We're in this together, as we saw when we talked about forgiveness, so our prayers can't be motivated by a narcissistic focus on self.

We are of infinite importance, but that doesn't mean the universe revolves around us.

Yes, God wants to bless us. But He doesn't want to us to be isolated. Our prayers, therefore, should be within a context of community.

That means not just praying for yourself, but praying for others. It means understanding that the blessings God gives you should be shared with others. It means praying with humility and love and understanding, as someone who looks out not only for their own interests, but also for the interests of others (Philippians 2:4). It means praying for God's will to be done first and foremost, not ours.

Prayer is relational, not transactional. We don't put in our devotional time and get answers back, as if prayer were some sort of payment for God's generosity. If we reduce prayer to a shopping list, we miss the point. Prayer is not meant to be about getting quick answers and going on our way, but about relationship and connection with God.

Maybe that's why the first line of the Lord's Prayer is about asking for God's will to be done. Jesus modeled this in the garden of Gethsemane, when He asked for "this cup," which referred to the suffering He knew was ahead, to be taken away from Him, but then added, "yet not my will, but yours be done" (Luke 22:42).

That's how we should pray. "God, I'd love this house or that job, I really would, and I'm praying for it and believing for it. But more than my desires, I want your will to be done."

The most effective prayers are the ones that are according to God's Word and His will. The least effective prayers are the ones that are according to our desires and will.

Prayer keeps us connected to God's will and to the needs of people around us. It grounds us. It keeps us from getting isolated.

6. BOOMERANG PRAYERS

Boomerang prayers are the kind of prayers you toss up to God but then catch again.

In other words, you "give all your worries and cares to God, for he cares about you" (1 Peter 5:7 NLT), but you don't leave your worries and cares there with Him; you pick them back up. You carry them around with you. You sleep with them at night, wake up with them in the morning, and take them to school or work during the day.

Prayer will only reduce your stress and worry if you are able to leave the things you're anxious about with God. You have to learn to trust Him, to rely on Him, to wait on Him.

It might be overstating it to call these prayers a waste of time because God is gracious and kind and good, and He helps us even when we think we are carrying the load ourselves. But when we pray boomerang prayers, we are missing out on some of the most important benefits of prayer, particularly the peace and perspective that prayer should bring.

Prayer will only reduce your stress and worry if you are able to leave the things you're anxious about with God.

There are times to think about and work toward solving problems, and there are times to recognize that only God can take those things from here. I'm sure you've read the Serenity Prayer, a short prayer that has been widely used in recovery programs (and printed on bookmarks and refrigerator magnets) for decades.

> God, grant me the serenity
> to accept the things I cannot change,

courage to change the things I can,
and wisdom to know the difference.

(Side note: The prayer is usually attributed to theologian Reinhold Niebuhr, although for years a heated and very public debate raged between Niebuhr's daughter, Elisabeth Sifton, and a Yale Law School researcher named Fred Shapiro regarding who actually wrote it.[5] I think that's ironic considering the prayer is about serenity. But anyway—it's a great prayer.)

Casting our cares upon God means knowing when to let go, when to trust that the matter is safe in God's hands, and that you have done your best. You can work and trust at the same time, of course.

But you can't *worry* and trust at the same time.

Often we are called to continue working toward a solution or doing what we can to make progress, but we are not meant to anguish over the process as if we were alone.

Prayer accomplishes the unique task of giving our worries to God while also discerning what part we continue to play. When we pray, we find peace, but we also receive renewed courage and wisdom to press on.

Cast your worries upon the Lord and leave them there. They are safe with Him.

7. OPPRESSOR PRAYERS

You've probably noticed that all of these "useless prayers" are less about what we pray and more about why we pray or who we are when no one is watching. This last one is no exception.

God will not hear our prayers if we are abusing or oppressing those we have power over, or if we are hurting people in our lives we should be caring for. Listen to what God says to Israel through Isaiah the prophet:

> When you spread out your hands in prayer,
> I hide my eyes from you;
> even when you offer many prayers,
> I am not listening.
> Your hands are full of blood!
> Wash and make yourselves clean.
> Take your evil deeds out of my sight;
> stop doing wrong.
> Learn to do right; seek justice.
> Defend the oppressed.
> Take up the cause of the fatherless;
> plead the case of the widow.
>
> Isaiah 1:15–17

God takes very seriously how we treat people around us. In particular, He watches how we behave toward those with less power and voice than us.

The fatherless and the widow represented groups of people who were essentially defenseless in that society, which was largely agricultural and highly patriarchal. Isaiah was reminding people that coming to God with eloquent prayers meant nothing if their hands were "full of blood." That is, if during the week they were mistreating people—such as their employees or the poor—they had no business showing up to the temple and lifting their hands in prayer.

Peter says something similar to husbands in the New Testament:

> Husbands, in the same way be considerate as you live with your wives, and treat them with respect as the weaker partner and as heirs with you of the gracious gift of life, so that nothing will hinder your prayers.
>
> 1 Peter 3:7

A husband's prayers will be "hindered" if he doesn't treat his wife respectfully, as a partner and co-heir of God's gifts.

Unfortunately, this verse has often been used to demean women by focusing on the word _weaker_. In reality, the message of this passage is the _equality_ of men and women, not their hierarchy. In a Greco-Roman society that treated women as inferiors, this was disruptive, to say the least.

I'm married to a strong woman who is fully my equal. There is nothing weak about her or any of the countless women I know. Let's get past the outdated idea of a "weaker sex," which is based in part on a misreading of this text.

The point isn't that women are inherently weaker. It's that a husband must use his power and privilege to _serve_, not to take; to _liberate_, not to dominate. I think it was a reference not to innate gender differences, but to gender stereotypes and cultural norms that made it nearly impossible for women to live independently. That wasn't their fault; it was society's fault. The culture was skewed against women. Culture had given men power and authority, and Peter was telling them to stop abusing that privilege and instead to see their wives (and by extension women in general) as equals.

Because God himself was watching.

Since Peter's time, a lot has changed, and yet at the same time very little has changed. Although women have more opportunities than they did two thousand years ago, they still face countless challenges that men do not. We aren't where we need to be as a society, and that includes the church. Men—in the home, in the church, and in society—are solemnly charged by God to treat the women in their lives as equals in every way.

The same goes for every other marginalized community around us.

As Christians, we have an obligation to live as Jesus did. He sought out and served poor people, lepers, sinners, thieves, widows, women, Samaritans, tax collectors, and societal outcasts. He served the rich, the religious, and the rulers too, but He didn't show them preference. If anything, He held them to a higher standard because of their power.

Jesus didn't reject anyone. Instead, He called everyone equally to love God above all and to love their neighbor as themselves.

What does this mean for us today? That God doesn't hear our prayers on Sunday if we are harming the people He loves Monday through Saturday. He won't listen to us if we are using our position or power to take rather than to give. If that is the case, His ear is open to *their* cry, not ours. We could actually make ourselves His enemies if we are hurting those with less power or voice than us.

That includes ethnic minorities, foreigners, marginalized communities, people with less economic or educational privilege, employees, those who struggle with addictions or mental illness, LGBTQ individuals, prisoners and ex-convicts, those whose body types don't fit the "ideal," those who find themselves home-less, immigrants, older adults, disabled people—and the list goes on indefinitely.

It doesn't matter whether we agree with their lifestyle choices or theology; we are called and commanded to love, serve, protect, and care for those around us. We are all God's family, and God loves us all equally. He asks us to do the same.

Love that is conditional is not love at all.

And prayers with blood on our hands are not prayers at all.

These seven useless prayers—

hypocritical prayers
babbling prayers
bitter prayers
complacent prayers
narcissistic prayers
boomerang prayers
oppressor prayers

—all highlight the same thing: God cares more about who we are than what we say. He lamented about Israel, "These people come near to me with their mouth and honor me with their lips, but their hearts are far from me" (Isaiah 29:13).

God is a gracious, generous God who hears us when we pray. Rest assured: God does want to listen to us. We don't have to approach Him in fear or guilt. We do, however, have to take seriously the motivations and behaviors that surround our prayers. We are speaking with God, after all, and He is holy, powerful, and perfect in every way.

King Solomon reminds us:

> Guard your steps when you go to the house of God. Go near to listen rather than to offer the sacrifice of fools, who do not know that they do wrong.
>
> > Do not be quick with your mouth,
> > do not be hasty in your heart
> > to utter anything before God.
> > God is in heaven
> > and you are on earth,
> > so let your words be few.
> >   Ecclesiastes 5:1–2

In other words, we need to be humble and teachable when we come into God's presence. He might want to address something under the surface that we didn't realize needed adjustment.

That's a good thing. God's correction is always to our benefit.

We can probably all admit that there have been times when our prayers have fallen into one or more of the above categories. But let's not stay there. Let's allow God to search our hearts, educate our minds, correct our steps, and empower our prayer lives.

You can eliminate useless prayers, starting now. And I don't know who else needs to hear this, but you can throw out that bag of single socks too.

---------- TWELVE ----------

The cycle of prayer

When I was a child, we couldn't afford a VCR. If you didn't grow up in the eighties, you can't know the full emotional impact of that statement. Today you can stream episodes of your favorite series on your watch while you're in the bathroom. Back then, though, options were far more limited, and a VCR was the gateway to childhood happiness. You could record things for later, watch the same movies over and over, or rent movies to watch with your friends—it was technological heaven.

One day, at a farmers' market, there was a raffle to win a VCR. I begged my mom to purchase a ticket because I knew that was my only shot at getting one. Honestly, there was very little chance of getting her to buy a raffle ticket either, but at least I could try.

I don't know if my mom secretly wanted a VCR or if she just couldn't resist my pleas, but she bought a ticket. The drawing wasn't for a few days, so every morning at breakfast, she would pull the ticket out and we would ask God for a VCR. My mom used the opportunity to teach me to pray and to have faith. She would quote Scriptures about prayer and encourage me to trust God.

I'll never forget the evening our home phone rang. I waited anxiously while my mom answered it. She started freaking out on the phone, and in that moment, I knew we had won the raffle.

Praying a few days for a VCR might seem like a short time to wait and a small thing to pray for. But for a kid, it was everything. That experience marked me, and it led me to believe God for crazy requests in prayer.

It also taught me the value of _persevering_ in prayer. Not just praying once, but persisting. Not giving up, but pressing in and pressing through.

My mom didn't promise me that God would give us the VCR, but she did promise me that God cared about my requests, that He heard my prayers, and that He answers prayers. She taught me to keep praying and believing. And when the answer came, she pointed everything straight back to God. She doubled down on the truth that God answers our prayers.

I've never forgotten her lesson.

NEVER GIVE UP

Persevering in prayer has always been a challenge for humans. Jesus' disciples were no exception. So Jesus decided to teach them about praying in faith even when they didn't see an immediate answer. Here is the story, told in Luke 18:1–8:

> Jesus told his disciples a parable to show them that they should always pray and not give up. He said: "In a certain town there was a judge who neither feared God nor cared what people thought. And there was a widow in that town who kept coming to him with the plea, 'Grant me justice against my adversary.'
>
> "For some time he refused. But finally he said to himself, 'Even though I don't fear God or care what people think, yet because this widow keeps bothering me, I will see that she gets justice, so that she won't eventually come and attack me!'"

> And the Lord said, "Listen to what the unjust judge says. And will not God bring about justice for his chosen ones, who cry out to him day and night? Will he keep putting them off? I tell you, he will see that they get justice, and quickly. However, when the Son of Man comes, will he find faith on the earth?"

To recap the parable: A vulnerable widow who was desperate for justice pestered a selfish judge until he finally did his job, and justice was done.

I love so many things about this story. First, notice that Jesus really *wanted* them to pray and not give up. He knew how easy it was to get discouraged or weary, so He specifically taught on the subject.

God doesn't hate it when we pray fervently and frequently; He loves it. He responds to it.

Second, I love how the woman is one of the most vulnerable people in that society: a widow. She didn't get justice because she had some sort of clout or leverage, or because she could give the judge a bribe, or because she was more important than other cases on his docket. She got justice because she asked for it repeatedly, unwaveringly, confidently.

God doesn't hate it when we pray fervently and frequently; He loves it. He responds to it.

In the same way, God doesn't answer prayers based on our merit. He doesn't play favorites either. He listens to prayers, and prayers move His heart and hand.

Third, it's fascinating that the judge is a jerk. Jesus intentionally describes him as the worst kind of judge: He doesn't obey God, he doesn't care about people, and he's unjust. He is the kind of judge that would have only responded to bribes or threats, not to pleas for mercy.

Obviously, God is not this way. That's the whole point here. Jesus is saying that if the worst judge imaginable would do justice for the least powerful person simply because *she asked without ceasing,* how much more will a *good* God respond to His *children?*

In other words, we have a lot going for us when we pray! God isn't against us. He isn't cold and unfeeling. He isn't waiting for a bribe. We aren't nameless faces in a courtroom. We aren't a bother or hindrance or distraction to Him. We are the focus of His infinite goodness.

Why would we *not* persevere in prayer?

When Jesus finished His story, I can imagine the disciples laughing at the widow's persistence and the judge's exasperation. The irony of a powerful judge being confounded by the persistence of a tiny widow would have stayed in their minds.

The point here is not just that there is power in persistence, but that *God is predisposed to help us*. The meaning of the parable hangs on the contrast between the unjust judge and our good God. We don't have to nag God into helping us, because He already wants to.

To Him, our prayers are not nagging at all. They are an expression of faith. They are heartfelt requests that He delights to fulfill.

Jesus is saying that when you pray, don't assume God won't answer—assume He will.

So ask away! Pray boldly for as long as it takes. God might be on the verge of answering the prayer right now. You never know when it could happen or what it will look like. It would be a tragedy to give up too soon.

You might be thinking, *You said God wouldn't hear us just because we use a lot of words. Now you're saying we should keep on praying as long as it takes. That's inconsistent!*

There is a big difference between trying to be heard because of our "many words," as Jesus said, and praying without giving up. The first treats God like a vending machine: If you put in enough prayer coins, an answer drops out of some heavenly chute. It's a transactional approach that treats prayer like a price or a debt that we have to fulfill before we can get what we want.

But as we saw earlier, prayer is relational, not transactional. We don't pray until we've paid a debt or earned our answer. We pray because we know God loves us and is listening.

Notice how Jesus connected answered prayer to God's goodness, not our efforts, in Matthew 7:7–11:

> Ask and it will be given to you; seek and you will find; knock and the door will be opened to you. For everyone who asks receives; the one who seeks finds; and to the one who knocks, the door will be opened.
>
> Which of you, if your son asks for bread, will give him a stone? Or if he asks for a fish, will give him a snake? If you, then, though you are evil, know how to give good gifts to your children, how much more will your Father in heaven give good gifts to those who ask him!

The difference between incessant babbling and persevering prayer is—as in almost every area of prayer—our heart attitude. The former tries to manipulate God into doing what we want by piling fancy phrases higher and higher like a game of spiritual Jenga. The latter patiently trusts God to do what is right and best, confident in His character and unworried by delay.

Most of us know the name of Apple's founder and iconic CEO, Steve Jobs. His partner, Steve Wozniak, is nearly as well known. Both made billions of dollars from the success of Apple.

There was a third founder, though, who is nearly always forgotten. When Apple was incorporated on April 2, 1976, an engineer named Ron Wayne owned a 10 percent stake in the company. A mere twelve days later, partly because he felt out of his league next to the two Steves, Ron sold his shares back for eight hundred dollars. Today, those shares would be worth billions.

Now in his eighties, Ron has a philosophical approach toward the decision. He doesn't bemoan the fact that he could be a billionaire. He knows why he made those choices in the moment, and he doesn't want to waste energy on regret.[1]

I can't second-guess poor Ron, of course. Money doesn't buy happiness anyway, as we all know. But you still have to wonder—what if he had found a way to stay in the game? If he had trusted the abilities of his partners rather than feeling intimidated by them? What if he hadn't given up after twelve days?

History is full of other almost-millionaires, almost-celebrities, almost-victors. Hindsight is always 20/20, so I'm not judging them, but that doesn't make their decisions any less agonizing.

At the same time, I wonder how many times I've given up too easily, too quickly, in my prayers. Have there been times when I've been unwilling to trust God, my senior partner, to carry me through? Have I stopped believing too soon?

I'm sure I have. Maybe you have too. That's why Jesus' words are for us today.

Always pray.

Never give up.

Call out day and night.

Let Jesus find faith, not doubt, in your heart.

ASK, WATCH, WAIT, REPEAT

The Old Testament prophet Elijah has a lot to teach us about persistent prayer. James used his life to illustrate how powerful it is when humans pray:

> The prayer of a righteous person is powerful and effective. Elijah was a human being, even as we are. He prayed earnestly that it would not rain, and it did not rain on the land for three and a half years. Again he prayed, and the heavens gave rain, and the earth produced its crops.
>
> 5:16–18

Elijah was a prophet sent to Israel when the nation was in a bad place. Evil, oppressive leadership had moved the nation away from God and from justice. As a way to get people to wake up and return to God, Elijah prayed that the rains would stop in Israel. From that day on, it didn't rain.

Three years later, God spoke to Elijah and said it was time for the drought to end. He was going to bring rain to the land. But first, Elijah needed to confront the nation about their idolatry and ask them to repent.

What followed was the most epic showdown imaginable between Elijah and the false religion of Baal worship that had captivated Israel. Essentially, Elijah challenged the priests of Baal to a divine duel. Their god didn't do a thing, of course. Then God sent fire from heaven, and Israel realized they needed to get their act together.

It still hadn't rained, but Elijah knew what God had promised. This is where the story really gets interesting.

There wasn't a cloud in the sky and it hadn't rained in three years, but Elijah told the king, Ahab, "There is the sound of a heavy rain" (1 Kings 18:41). Ahab probably raised his eyebrows at that crazy statement, but he had just seen Elijah call down fire from heaven, so he wasn't about to argue.

The story continues. Elijah climbed up a mountain, "bent down to the ground and put his face between his knees" (verse 42). I know that sounds like a yoga position, but it was a posture of prayer. It's one you won't ever find me using because I'm in my forties and not as flexible as I used to be, but Elijah was an amazing guy. And apparently very fit.

It's fascinating to me that Elijah's response to the promise of God was to pray. He knew God was in charge, but he also realized he had a part to play in the process. Not a huge part, granted, because he was as human as you and me, and therefore couldn't control weather patterns—but an important part, nonetheless. So he prayed.

And nothing happened. No rain. No wind. No clouds.

Elijah sent his servant to look toward the Mediterranean Sea, sparkling in the distance. He was expecting to see a storm on the horizon, but the servant told him, "There is nothing there" (verse 43).

Elijah was not discouraged. He repeated this seven times. _Seven._ I can only guess what the servant was thinking as his master, with his head between his knees, prayed like crazy and insisted that it was going to start pouring any minute now.

The seventh time, the servant saw something. He came running back. "A cloud as small as a man's hand is rising from the sea" (verse 44).

I imagine the servant holding his fist straight out and measuring the width of the cloud against it. Try it yourself. Now imagine yourself on a parched desert mountaintop, looking at a white fuzzball the size of your fist forming in the hot, clear sky.

The exact size would have depended on the distance. But no matter how you imagine it, it's still pretty underwhelming.

You can almost hear the disdain in the servant's tone. "Um, sir, yes, there is a cloud over there. A teeny, insignificant, cute little cloud. But it's nothing to get too excited about. It's probably going to blow away in the wind. It hasn't rained for three years, after all. . . ."

But Elijah was already on his feet, shouting in triumph. He told the servant to warn the king, "Hitch up your chariot and go down before the rain stops you" (verse 44).

The story continues: "Meanwhile, the sky grew black with clouds, the wind rose, a heavy rain started falling and Ahab rode off to Jezreel. The power of the Lord came on Elijah and, tucking his cloak into his belt, he ran ahead of Ahab all the way to Jezreel" (verses 45–46).

I told you he was fit.

The point of this passage is not Elijah's flexibility or athletic prowess. It's his persistence in prayer. That's what James highlighted centuries later, and it's what still speaks to us today.

Notice the cycle of prayer that Elijah followed:

> He asked God for rain.
>
> He watched to see if there was an answer.
>
> He waited on God.
>
> Then he prayed again.

Ask, watch, wait, repeat. It's the cycle of prayer.

Notice what Elijah *didn't* do: He didn't quit. He prayed earnestly, continually, and with faith until he saw the answer.

Remember, this was something God had promised. Elijah could have said, "If it's God's will, He'll do it without my involvement. He doesn't need me." He could have complained, "I prayed, but God didn't keep His end of the deal." He could have concluded, "Maybe I didn't hear from God after all."

Elijah did none of those things. He just kept praying.

That is exactly the kind of persistent prayer Jesus taught about. When we go to God in prayer, we shouldn't be easily discouraged. We can't assume that just because we don't get a quick answer, the answer is no.

Take a cue from small children. They have no problem asking the same thing over and over, ad infinitum. Trust me, I speak from experience.

Ask God again. And again. And again. Ask Him in faith, trusting that He cares about you and is predisposed to help you.

What do you have to lose?

Sometimes you will hear a clear no. Sometimes you'll just know in your heart that you don't need to pray anymore. Sometimes you'll realize your prayers need to be tweaked or redirected because they are wrong prayers. Sometimes they might fall into one of the categories we looked at in the last chapter.

But assuming none of those things are true, keep praying! Pray until God makes it clear you should stop.

We'll talk more about unanswered prayer later on, but remember this: Prayers nearly always feel unanswered at first. That's the challenge of waiting. Even if it's a four-day wait for a VCR, the cycle of asking, watching, and waiting can be discouraging if you aren't prepared for it.

Pray until God makes it clear you should stop.

That's where the faith of Elijah comes in. That's where you need to be inspired by the widow who took down a judge. That's when God wants to whisper into your heart to pray without ceasing, to believe Him for the impossible, to cast your cares on Him because He cares for you.

Your persistence reveals your faith, and your faith moves the heart of God.

THIRTEEN

Spiritual bypassing is not spiritual at all

A while back, a friend of mine killed her car.

The worst part is that it was a beautiful Mercedes-Benz; not brand-new or anything, but one of those cars that are timelessly cool, with real personality. Everybody loved it. That made its tragic passing even more painful.

Here's how it happened. My friend had recently moved to LA from the South, with a cute Southern accent and a head full of dreams.

Apparently her focus was on her dreams, though, not the oil level in her car.

When the "check oil" light first appeared, it was intermittent. But eventually it stayed on permanently, a glowing red alert on the instrument panel every time she drove. She didn't think too much of it, though. Her dad had always taken care of things like that. She hoped that if she ignored it long enough, it would fix itself.

This went on for months. The light stayed on, forlornly trying to warn her that the engine needed attention. Needless to say, ignoring the problem didn't work, and the car didn't fix itself.

She drove that innocent Mercedes-Benz right into oblivion.

There was no funeral. Too bad, because we all would have attended.

RIP Mercedes-Benz.

We still give my friend a hard time about her naiveté. But I wonder, how often do we do the same thing when it comes to problems in our minds and emotions? We ignore warning signs and hope that our traumas and dramas will fix themselves.

> **It's easier to pray about things than to actually put in the work to fix them.**

Even worse, we often use spiritual language to cover up deep issues. We don't do this intentionally, at least for the most part. But it's easier to pray about things than to actually put in the work to fix them.

This does a disservice to prayer, and it sets us up for failure. Yes, we should pray about everything, but that doesn't mean prayer alone will fix everything. It was never meant to be a cure-all, a magic potion that would make all pain go away with no effort on our part.

> Prayer should accompany action, not replace it.
> Prayer should bring pain points to light, not hide them.
> Prayer should facilitate healing, not enable continued abuse.
> Prayer should empower and direct our efforts, not excuse our laziness.

"JUST PRAY ABOUT IT"

The tendency to use prayer and other spiritual practices or beliefs to avoid doing real work has a name. It's called _spiritual bypassing._

The term originated in the field of psychology. Psychologist and professor Dr. Philip Clark defines it as "the avoidance of underlying emotional issues by focusing solely on spiritual beliefs, practices, and experiences."[1]

In other words, spiritual bypassing means that instead of paying the price to understand and fix things that are out of alignment in your thoughts and emotions, you try to cover up the issues and move on by "praying about it," or "just having faith," or something similar.

We do this more than we probably realize.

It can be difficult to identify spiritual bypassing, though. After all, we should turn to prayer when we feel overwhelmed. That's the premise of the "pray about everything, be anxious about nothing" verse. No matter what needs or problems we face, whether little or big, the Bible tells us to pray, have faith, and trust God.

Is that spiritual bypassing?

No. Well, not in and of itself.

Prayer is not the problem. We should always pray. The problem is when we don't take personal responsibility for what *we* need to do. The moment we use prayer, faith, Bible, church, tithing, God, heaven, or any other spiritual belief or practice to avoid personal responsibility, we've crossed the line into spiritual bypassing.

On a practical level, what does spiritual bypassing look like? Usually, it means substituting internal growth or tangible action with a cheap appeal to:

- Prayer: "Just pray about it."
- Faith: "If you just had more faith . . ."
- Heaven: "This earth is sinful and broken; all will be made right in heaven."
- God's sovereignty: "His ways are higher than ours, so don't try to understand."
- Spiritual disciplines: "If you would give/fast/volunteer, you would be blessed."
- Forgiveness: "You have to forgive, forget, and move on."
- Unity: "If you disagree or complain, you're causing division."

- Vision: "I know you're suffering, but you are part of something bigger, so it's worth it."
- Love: "Love covers a multitude of sins; love keeps no record of wrongs."

The difficult thing with spiritual bypassing is that it sounds so, well, *spiritual*. It's hard to object when the person doing the bypassing is quoting the Bible or appealing to your generous, compassionate nature. The bulleted list above consists of good things, after all. And most of the phrases in quotes come from the Bible or can be supported biblically.

The difference, though, is how they are being used. Are we quoting the Bible and talking about spiritual things in order to serve others and to follow God wholeheartedly? Or are we using them to avoid change, escape accountability, or control people?

These are important questions to answer because God is not impressed with fake spirituality. He is not manipulatable, and He doesn't take kindly to people manipulating other people in His name. He also doesn't want us to deceive ourselves into thinking we are healthy, happy, and holy just because we checked off our spiritual to-do list this morning. This sort of superficial, religious whitewashing was what got the Pharisees into trouble with Jesus regularly.

THE MORE IMPORTANT MATTERS

The term *spiritual bypassing* is relatively new, but the action it describes is as old as humanity.

James writes, "Suppose a brother or a sister is without clothes and daily food. If one of you says to them, 'Go in peace; keep warm and well fed,' but does nothing about their physical needs, what good is it?" (2:15–16).

Note that phrase: "Go in peace; keep warm and well fed." That is some James-level sarcasm, and I'm here for it.

And yet, we do this exact thing when we substitute prayer for action, empty faith for generosity, religious platitudes for practical love.

The prophets frequently confronted Israel for their tendency to bypass needed social change with religious activity. The people would offer sacrifices, pray, and claim to follow God, all the while ignoring the real issues around them, which included taking care of the poor, standing up for the oppressed, and making sure justice was done in the legal system.

For example, the prophet Hosea says, "For I desire mercy, not sacrifice, and acknowledgment of God rather than burnt offerings" (6:6).

Micah says something very similar: "He has shown you, O mortal, what is good. And what does the LORD require of you? To act justly and to love mercy and to walk humbly with your God" (6:8).

God's value system is not based on saying the right words or meeting some religious expectation, but on *being the right kind of people*. We are meant to reflect the love, mercy, and justice that characterize Him.

Hundreds of years later, Jesus called out the Pharisees for doing the same thing. "Woe to you, teachers of the law and Pharisees, you hypocrites! You give a tenth of your spices—mint, dill and cumin. But you have neglected the more important matters of the law—justice, mercy and faithfulness. You should have practiced the latter, without neglecting the former" (Matthew 23:23).

Notice the phrase, "the more important matters." Jesus was saying that they were nitpicking over the tiniest details, all the way down to tithing the herbs that grew in their gardens, but they were ignoring what really mattered. Justice. Mercy. Faithfulness.

The point of the phrase, "more important matters," is to make us think about what we are spending our time and energy on doing well. Are we doing the small things right but the big things wrong?

In other words, if your Mercedes-Benz has a "check oil" light flashing at you, don't just wash and polish the outside of the car. You take it in for service.

None of us are perfect, but we should always pay the most attention to the areas that are most important.

WHOLE PEOPLE ARE HEALTHY PEOPLE

Spiritual bypassing comes from a mindset that sees our spirit as separate from the rest of our selves. We think that belief in God means ignoring the physical, tangible parts of our beings in favor of spiritual practices.

But it doesn't work that way. You can't separate the pieces of yourself.

Faith doesn't exist separately. Our spirituality, and therefore our prayers, are inextricably connected to every aspect of who we are: mind, soul, spirit, body, will, emotion.

Dr. Clark writes:

> One key identifier of spiritual bypass is an obvious imbalance or compartmentalization of the self; rather than integrating all levels of human consciousness, those in spiritual bypass focus solely on the spiritual level as a means to avoid painful psychological work. . . . The spiritual practices, seeking, and focus are not in and of themselves detrimental. Rather, the concern is the avoidance of the psychological and emotional work that is necessary for healing. Therefore, the discourse around spiritual bypass does not carry the implication that the spiritual life is wrong or unhealthy. There are times, however, when the most appropriate spiritual practice is to engage in necessary, albeit uncomfortable, psychological work.[2]

In other words, we need spiritual practices—but we also need to deal with trauma. We need to understand grief. We need to recognize our weaknesses, addictions, fears, and dreams. We need to take care of our entire selves: body, soul, and spirit.

So yes, have faith for physical health. But also eat more salads and fewer corn dogs.

Pray for your finals. But also study and get a good night's sleep.

Ask God to bless your finances. But read a book or take a class or at least watch a few YouTube videos about balancing a budget.

Faith and works are friends. And they are on the same side—yours. Don't pit them against each other. Beware of teaching or philosophies that deny reality in the name of faith or that permit abuse to continue under the guise of spirituality.

There is nothing spiritual about ignoring reality. Faith is not blind. Only foolishness is.

I remember an old preacher saying that he had met people who were "so heavenly minded they were no earthly good." He makes a valid point. If your faith doesn't work in the real world, maybe it's not faith at all. Maybe it's escapism.

Real faith is fully aware of what is happening in the physical world, but it sees beyond that world. It takes God into account. It uses faith to inform the present, not deny it.

Your faith should make you more whole, not more fragmented. It should align you, orient you, stabilize you, unify you. If it doesn't, get a new one, because yours is broken.

THE SNEAKY DYNAMICS OF BYPASSING

Religious bypassing is a sneaky thing. As I said before, we do it without realizing it—not from a bad heart, but rather from a subconscious desire to skip over the difficult work we need to be doing.

As Jeremiah wrote, "The heart is deceitful above all things and beyond cure. Who can understand it? 'I the LORD search the heart and examine the mind'" (17:9–10).

We need God to unmask and unpack the hidden motivations of our hearts. Let's look in more detail at some of the reasons we might engage in spiritual bypassing, particularly with regard to prayer.

1. To avoid dealing with our own pain and trauma

I mentioned in an earlier chapter that one of the great benefits of prayer is that it helps us process pain, trouble, and trauma. Don't use prayer to cover up pain—use it to deal with it. To explore it. To find areas where you need additional resources or help.

Don't let anyone tell you that your depression would go away, or you would overcome addiction if you "just had more faith." They don't know your faith level. Only God does. Yes, faith is essential, and prayer is always helpful. But there are some things in life that take wisdom, understanding, and hard work.

2. To avoid feeling someone else's pain

Be careful not to reply too quickly, "I'll pray for you," or, "You should pray about that." First, sit with their pain. Understand their question or concern. Be wary of the human tendency to keep other people's pain at arm's length. Once you've truly entered into their world, once you've engaged empathy and compassion, then prayer is usually appropriate (and better received).

Again, though, don't limit your response to prayer alone if there is something more you can do.

3. To avoid hard work

Prayer, faith, heaven, and God are all invisible. Difficult to measure. Subjective. As a result, there is little immediate accountability, and we can deceive ourselves into thinking that we are doing our part.

It's easier to pray about getting a job than to go out and get one. It's less vulnerable to pray for a spouse than to ask someone out on a date. It's more comfortable to stay at home and complain about not having friends than to put yourself out there and make friends.

On a wider level, spiritual bypassing could include refusing to address social problems because "the only answer is Jesus," or, "only heaven is free from pain or suffering." Or not caring for this planet as we should because "there's going to be a new heaven and a new earth anyway."

Prayer is wonderful— but praying when you should be obeying is a problem.

There is a story in the Old Testament about how King Saul—who was not a good king on any level—disobeyed a particular command from God and then claimed he was doing it so he could offer sacrifices to God. The prophet Samuel was not impressed. He said, "Does the LORD delight in burnt offerings and sacrifices as much as in obeying the LORD? To obey is better than sacrifice, and to heed is better than the fat of rams" (1 Samuel 15:22).

The parallel to prayer and other spiritual activity should be clear. When God asks us to take action, He expects *action*, not prayer, praise, fasting, church attendance, or any other spiritual activity.

Prayer is wonderful—but praying when you should be obeying is a problem.

4. To protect the status quo

When someone is pointing out something that is broken in the systems around them, or when they are sharing their story of hurt or abuse, spiritual bypassing can look like a quick appeal to "love," or "unity," or "the greater good."

This can easily happen in church or in the home. If we are leaders in these spaces, we need to take time to hear the complaints around us and make needed changes, not sweep them under the rug in the name of "all the good things that are happening."

5. To shift the responsibility

"I'm praying, so it's in God's hands. He knows where I live. I'm just trusting Him and waiting on His perfect timing." That sounds so spiritual, right? And maybe it is. Or maybe it's just spiritual bypassing. You have to be able to tell the difference. Usually, if we're honest with ourselves, deep down inside we know when we are ignoring the check oil light in our lives.

6. To excuse or minimize our mistakes

It's human nature to want to blame someone when things go wrong. And it's also human nature to want to avoid being the one blamed. So we look to God or the devil as convenient scapegoats.

The most famous excuse in this category is, "The devil made me do it." I think most of us see through that. But then we say things like, "God could have stopped me, but He didn't." Or, "God works all things together for good, including my mistakes." True . . . but it's not the ideal scenario to work with, that's for sure. And there are still going to be consequences when we make mistakes.

Yes, we should trust in God's sovereignty. Yes, we should forgive ourselves and move on when we mess up. Yes, God uses even the evil things for our good. But those truths don't invalidate the fact that we are responsible for our decisions.

If you've messed up, you need to make it right to the best of your ability. That means coming clean about what you did, apologizing to the offended parties, making restitution if you can, and making real changes so you don't repeat the mistake.

Don't say, "God sees my heart," or, "Only God is perfect," if you're using those phrases to excuse your mistakes.

7. To justify ongoing bad behavior

People sometimes use the Bible or spiritual principles to enable their inappropriate behavior. This might be the most dangerous reason of all because of its potential for deep, ongoing hurt.

This can include gaslighting, victim-blaming, or other forms of manipulation couched in spiritual terms. An example of this is an authority figure demanding that people forgive them repeatedly, insisting on "grace" and "mercy" rather than making amends and changing, or blaming their wrong behavior on others rather than owning it.

We must make sure that we are not weaponizing our faith to protect ourselves or take advantage of others, even inadvertently. The Bible, faith, prayer, and church communities exist to serve people, not to control them. God takes this very seriously, as we have seen in the writings of James, Hosea, Micah, and others.

In all of this, we must remain open to the conviction of the Holy Spirit. Just because we use Christian words or go to church or quote verses from the Bible doesn't mean we are acting with a pure heart.

Prayer is one of the best ways to keep our hearts clean and our motivations pure before God. He sees the secret recesses of the heart, and He will bring to our attention things that could become pitfalls for us or sources of pain for others.

These seven hidden motivations—hiding our pain, dismissing the pain of others, avoiding hard work, protecting the status quo, shifting responsibility, excusing mistakes, and justifying ongoing bad behavior—are not doing us any good. They are just covering up the real issues. If left unchecked, they could lead to serious problems down the road.

God is faithful to allow "check oil" moments in your life because He cares about your health and about those around you. Those might look like people complaining to you. They might look like anxiety or depression. They might look like broken relationships. They might look like financial problems.

Don't ignore the warning lights of your heart. Don't use prayer or faith or love to mask what's really going on. Don't drive your soul into oblivion—that's far more tragic than killing a Mercedes-Benz.

Instead, use prayer, faith, love, and every other spiritual tool at your disposal to dig deeper into what is really going on, and then get to work on it. Get advice or counseling. Study and learn. Grow in wisdom. Listen to people around you, and listen to the Holy Spirit. Humble yourself and begin to grow.

God will bring change and healing if you're willing to put in the work.

FOURTEEN

The dark side of prayer

Do you remember trying to spot the man in the moon when you were a kid? Here in LA, the moon and a handful of stars are usually all we can see, thanks to pollution and light glare, so finding the man in the moon is the extent of my astronomical goals.

Maybe you've noticed that regardless of how illuminated the moon is, the man in the moon's face is always there. Well, part of it, anyway. That's because the moon doesn't spin quickly, as Earth does, but rather it's stuck facing us as it moves around our planet, like a phone on a selfie stick. That means you're always looking at the same side of the moon, no matter what day of the year you look or where you're located.

So what about the *other* side of the moon? The far side, the half we never see? That is often referred to as "the dark side of the moon," which also happens to be the title of a famous Pink Floyd album from the seventies.

I'm not sure what Pink Floyd meant by their title, but when it comes to the moon, "dark" does *not* mean "never illuminated." That was news to me when I heard it, so don't feel stupid if you assumed the dark side of the moon was always in literal darkness. Or maybe we should just feel stupid together.

Dark, in this case, means "hidden from view or knowledge."

I did a little reading on the subject. No humans have ever landed on the dark side of the moon. Only one spacecraft has, at least successfully, and that wasn't until 2019. A handful of humans have orbited the moon and seen the far side, and we have quite a few photos, but that's about it.[1]

It's quite fascinating, actually, that sixty-plus years into the space age, there is so much we don't know about something as close and supposedly familiar as the moon.

You could say the same thing about prayer. Or more specifically, about how God responds to prayer.

There is so much we don't know about prayer, about God, and about faith.

When it comes to God, there is—and always will be—a great deal of mystery. There is an unknown side, a hidden side, a "dark" side if you will, to prayer.

That is not a bad thing.

If we could reduce God to a science textbook, if we could describe Him, explain Him, and predict Him, He wouldn't be God. And if we turned prayer into a hocus-pocus, abracadabra-style incantation, it wouldn't be prayer.

God cannot be contained by humans. Prayer is not a way to control God but a reminder that He is beyond our control.

Remember Simon the sorcerer trying to pay Peter money in exchange for the power of the Holy Spirit? If you haven't read the story, it's found in Acts 8. Peter was in Samaria preaching. Simon was a local magician and warlock who was amazed at the miracles he saw happening. Simon assumed that if he paid enough, he could purchase the spells or knowledge to do those things himself.

Peter was not amused. He practically yelled at him, "May your money perish with you, because you thought you could buy the gift of God with money!" (Acts 8:20).

Humans haven't changed much. We still dream about genie-in-the-bottle scenarios that give us access to infinite wealth and total control over the process.

But God won't fit into a bottle. Or a magic lamp. Or a sorcerer's spell book. Or a pastor's systematic theology book. Or a church building. Or any other human-made container.

By definition, God is always beyond human understanding. Isaiah famously said, "As the heavens are higher than the earth, so are my ways higher than your ways and my thoughts than your thoughts" (Isaiah 55:9).

It would be irresponsible, even dangerous, to claim that God always makes sense or that prayers always get results. Some prayers will never be answered. Good people will go through bad things. Justice will not always be done.

This reality has to be addressed if we are going to have a lifestyle of prayer. We must have a mature perspective of the mystery and sovereignty of God, or we'll find ourselves discouraged or angry when we can't make everything make sense.

It doesn't make sense to *us* because we aren't God. God is not confused about anything that is going on.

When we get to heaven, we're going to have a better perspective on things. Paul wrote in 1 Corinthians 13, "For we know in part and we prophesy in part, but when completeness comes, what is in part disappears" (verses 9–10). I think he was saying that we can't be totally sure about anything while we are here on earth. We do our best, but ultimately, we realize many things are reserved for God, for heaven, and for eternity.

Religion (in the empty, human-created sense of the word) wants to eliminate mystery. It claims to have things figured out. It tries to turn God into a system and reduce faith to a formula.

Prayer does the opposite. It doesn't remove God's mystery. Instead, it puts us into the story of His mystery.

PRAYER IS CLOSENESS AND RESPECT

One way that prayer puts us into the mystery of God is by reminding us that He is God, and we are not. In other ways, it puts us in our place. What "place" is that? It's a place of both _closeness_ and _respect_.

I was raised on the West Coast, which is an entirely different culture from the South. Where I come from, it's fine to respond to your parents with a simple yes or no. You could even get away with something more casual: _sure, yeah, okay, nah, nope._

If you grew up in the South, though, it's a different story. You probably learned that the only acceptable answers to parental questions were _yes, sir; yes, ma'am; no, sir;_ or _no, ma'am._ Anything more casual than that could endanger life or limb. Why? Because they were your parents, and you'd better talk to them with respect. Or else.

I'm not going to argue for one culture over the other. Actually, they both have something to teach us. Familiar language implies closeness and trust, while more formal language implies respect. Both are good, and both are needed.

Closeness and respect are not mutually exclusive, of course. Whether you say _sir_ or _sure_, you can respect and honor your parents and simultaneously trust them, lean on them, laugh with them.

The same goes for God. Prayer should bring us closer to God, but it should also inspire awe and respect.

The love of God and the greatness of God go together. We love Him, but we also worship Him. We run into His presence, but we also realize that He is King, that we are running into the throne room of heaven. We have great confidence and access as His children, but we remember that our Father is the God of the universe.

Prayer creates both absolute trust and humble dependency. That's a great place to be. It's healthy, it's restful, it's honest.

The problem with unchecked religious systems is that they tend to replace closeness with protocol and respect with fear. Our relationship with God becomes more about walking on eggshells and less about coming confidently before His throne of grace. We begin to see God as distant, not close to us. And we're okay with that, because why would we want to be close to someone we're scared of?

True prayer upends the toxicity of empty religion. It creates closeness and awe at the same time.

Think about the last time you prayed from your heart, with urgency and rawness. Maybe you heard about a family member who was sick, or you lost your job, or you were facing serious financial pressure, or you found yourself spiraling into anxiety or depression. How did you talk to God in those moments?

Probably very directly. I'm guessing you didn't sound super "spiritual." You simply cried out to Him in desperation, maybe even anger, because you needed His help.

When we pray, we connect directly with God. We skip the artificial protocols of empty religious systems. We bypass human-made rules about how to approach God, and we burst into His presence with a confidence and humility He adores.

True prayer is *anti*-religious. Our raw, unfiltered, unpoliced conversations with God rebel against legalistic attempts to define and predict (and therefore control) God.

The more we pray, the closer we get to God and the more we are in awe of Him.

PRAYER IS THE LANGUAGE OF GRIEF

A second way that prayer puts us into the mystery of God is by giving us a way to lament. *Lament* is not a word you hear very often today, but it has always been a part of Jewish and Christian beliefs, and many other religions as well. There is even a book in the Bible named Lamentations.

I remember as if it were yesterday when my beloved Seattle SuperSonics moved to Oklahoma in 2008. Actually, they didn't just move—they were stolen. And it cut deep. It still does, to be honest. When it happened, I went through my own personal book of Lamentations. I felt mad, sad, betrayed, lied to, crushed, numb, and a thousand other things all at once.

That is lament. And that is sports. Funny how often they go together.

Expressing our grief to God is one of the most spiritual things we can do. It doesn't feel that way—it feels like venting. It feels like blasphemy, almost, to tell God what we really think and feel.

Some people never do it because they've been taught to only approach God with carefully curated words of prayer. But God already sees your heart. Why not express what you are feeling with your mouth? God is not afraid of those feelings. He created them, after all; and Jesus felt them too.

Historian and author Ernest Kurtz writes that to "experience sadness, despair, tears, and howls of pain demonstrates not some violation or deficit of spirituality, but rather the ultimate spirituality of acceptance."[2]

> **Expressing our grief to God is one of the most spiritual things we can do.**

Grief is its own form of prayer. It might have words, it might not. It might be expressed toward God, or it might simply be the overflow of a broken heart.

God cares about our grief. He sees it and hears it, and He weeps with us. David wrote, "The LORD is close to the brokenhearted and saves those who are crushed in spirit" (Psalm 34:18).

God doesn't wait for an invitation to draw close. Like a parent hearing the cry of a hurt child, He comes to us in our time of need.

That is good because prayer can be difficult in times of grief. We might feel like God himself is to blame for our suffering, that He let us down instead of saving us. We can be so overwhelmed that we are hardly able to put words together.

We often come to know God best in grief. The distractions and superficial things fade away, and we are left with the knowledge that God is real, and He is with us, and He cares. Nothing else makes sense, and we can't even explain what we know about God. All we know is that His presence and peace fill our hearts, fill the room, fill our day.

If you are going through something difficult and don't feel like praying, that's okay. Don't put yourself under pressure to act spiritual or pretend to have faith. Your grief is a prayer, and your sorrow is a cry to God. Just let Him love you. Let Him bring you peace and comfort. It's what He does best.

PRAYER IS REST

A third way that prayer puts us into the mystery of God is by bringing us to a place of rest. That might seem odd at first because "not knowing" seems like it should produce unease and anxiety, not rest. When we embrace the mystery of God, though, we discover the rest that comes from simply letting Him be God.

Have you ever watched a movie with someone who can't handle not knowing what is about to happen? Maybe it's one of those movies where the screenwriter purposefully makes things confusing, and the loose ends don't get tied up until the end. But your friend can't appreciate that artistic choice, so they pepper you with questions throughout the movie. As if you know any better than they do about what is going on. Finally, you snarl semi-seriously, "Just be quiet and enjoy the movie. It'll make sense later, I promise."

God doesn't snarl at us. He is patient with our questions too. But I think sometimes He rolls His eyes a bit and wishes we would just enjoy the mystery. He whispers, "It'll make sense later, I promise."

It's exhausting to have to have all the answers, isn't it? To try to keep everything under control, to foresee all the worst-case scenarios, to have multiple
backup plans for everything? Frankly, it's not just exhausting.

It's impossible.

Humans weren't built to be gods. We are made in the image of God, so we
have a degree of foresight, wisdom, and intelligence. There is a lot we can
do, and as we learned from James, part of faith is doing what we can do. But
part of faith is also accepting what only *God* can do.

The quest for full knowledge or control leads to burnout and anxiety, but
acceptance leads to rest. I'm not talking about giving up, but about giving
lordship over to God, about casting our cares on Him because He cares for
us (1 Peter 5:7).

Let the uncertainty of life lead you closer to God. Take His yoke upon you,
as Jesus invited His listeners to do, and you'll find rest for your soul.

PRAYER IS WONDER

Finally, prayer puts us into the mystery of God by awakening wonder. David
wrote, "I praise you because I am fearfully and wonderfully made; your
works are wonderful, I know that full well" (Psalm 139:14).

If something is *wonderful* it is admirable, marvelous, worthy of praise. The
word refers to the object in question. God is wonderful, the universe is
wonderful, grace is wonderful, humans are wonderful, love is wonderful,
family is wonderful . . . the list could go on forever.

To have a sense of wonder, though, refers to the subject: to the person who is
in awe of something else. As humans, we need to develop our gift of wonder.
I think God loves it when we stand in awe of a sunset, when we gaze at a
sleeping baby and feel overwhelmed with love, when we enjoy a meal with
friends, when we laugh at dumb memes online. The list of things we should
enjoy and love and laugh at could also go on forever.

Some of us spend more energy on cynicism than wonder, and it shows.

Prayer brings us back to childlike wonderment. First, because it reminds us how big God is and how much we need Him. Second, because when we are in God's presence, we can't help but be filled with joy and awe. And third, because answered prayer reminds us that there is an infinite, all-powerful God who cares about the details of our lives.

Prayer brings us back to childlike wonderment.

We will never figure God out, but that's okay. We don't need to. Divinity is above our pay grade anyway.

Instead, let's lean in to the mystery. Let's find closeness there, and awe of God, and comfort in our grief, and rest from worry, and wonder and joy.

Let's explore the "dark side" of God. Faith doesn't have to be certain to be faith. Prayer doesn't have to make sense to connect us with heaven. God doesn't have to be explained before we find peace in Him.

There is always more to learn about God.

In the last few chapters, we've looked at a few things we often "get wrong" about prayer. These are areas that are easily overlooked, misunderstood, or forgotten.

We talked about obstacles to prayer, prayers that are wasting our time, why we need to persevere in prayer, what spiritual bypassing is (and why it's not spiritual at all), and the mysterious, "dark" side of prayer. If your prayer life isn't what you want it to be, it's possible one or more of these areas could be to blame.

The last thing I would want, though, is for this overview of potential negatives to scare you away from prayer. Fixating on the mistakes or the dangers of something can do more harm than good. It's like when you Google symptoms of an illness and suddenly start to feel aches and pains that weren't there before. (Don't act like you haven't done that. We all have.)

So please don't be even a little bit intimidated by prayer. Don't worry about how good you are at it (what does that even mean, anyway?), how many minutes a day you pray, how many verses you quote, or how many names you know for God.

Just talk to Him.

The best way to learn to pray is simply to do it. That's the focus of the next chapters.

SECTION 3

GETTING BETTER AT PRAYER

Have you ever decided you wanted to learn a brand-new skill that was way outside your comfort zone, and it turned out to be easy? Learning a foreign language, maybe, or ballroom dancing, or surfing, or simply touching your toes after age forty?

Yeah, me neither.

Mastering a new skill is never easy, elegant, or quick. The never-ending supply of fail videos on YouTube bears witness to that.

For some reason, we don't usually expect the learning curve to be that steep. We think we should be able to pick up something new quickly, that our improvement should be obvious, and that setbacks won't happen.

This tends to happen with prayer too. We think prayer should be something we can master quickly. When we don't excel at it—maybe we get distracted, tired, discouraged, or bored—we mentally berate ourselves.

I should be better at this, we think. *I'm unspiritual, undisciplined, and exceptionally terrible at this whole praying thing. Jesus gave His life for me, and I fall asleep after three minutes of talking to Him.*

But can I be real for a second here? Prayer is talking with an invisible Being who may or may not respond in the moment. Sometimes it's going to feel weird. Or hard. Or boring.

When I pray, I find that doubts, distractions, and to-do lists interject themselves into my mind with the persistence of a toddler begging for my iPhone. If there were a YouTube compilation of prayer fails, I'm sure I'd be on it.

It may take some time to get to the place you want to be. And that's okay. It doesn't mean you are unspiritual or a bad Christian or a flake. It means you are human.

I think God is just fine with us being human. After all, we are His idea. He gave us our attention span (or lack thereof). He knows we have doubts. He knows we get tired. Jesus' own disciples took a power nap instead of praying with Jesus the night He got arrested.

Like any skill, though, you can benefit from studying and learning. That is the point of this section: to give you tools, techniques, and templates to help you pray better.

In the following chapters, we'll look at several helpful topics, including how to use the Lord's Prayer as a prayer model, "dangerous" prayers that truly change things, a "prayer menu" that explains the different types of prayer, suggestions for hearing from God, and finally a simple template for prayer that we use in our church.

Enjoy the journey of learning to pray, even if it isn't as quick or smooth as your perfectionistic side would like. Reject the temptation to judge yourself against others or your own expectations. There is no set of rules to follow, no pattern to which you must conform. After all, prayer isn't fundamentally a set of techniques to be mastered anyway.

It's communication with God.

It's a shared experience.

It's relationship.

FIFTEEN

Lord, teach us to bowl

Jesus' prayer life was so powerful, so moving, so real, that the ones closest to Him—His disciples—wanted to know how to pray like He did.

Luke records the moment in his gospel: "One day Jesus was praying in a certain place. When he finished, one of his disciples said to him, 'Lord, teach us to pray, just as John taught his disciples'" (11:1).

So Jesus did. He gave them what we now call the Lord's Prayer.

Stop and think about that for a second. Jesus didn't write manuals or rule books. He rarely made lists. He liked to tell stories, ask tough questions, and ruffle people's feathers. He particularly seemed to enjoy baiting His disciples—when they came to Him with questions or complaints, He almost never gave them an easy answer.

When they asked Jesus to teach them how to pray, though, He did just that. He stopped what He was doing and laid out a simple model to follow. It wasn't a formula or a ritual prayer to memorize and recite. It wasn't a checklist.

It was a template: an example of how to pray that the disciples could use as they learned to communicate with God through prayer.

If you've ever used a template to create a PowerPoint presentation or draft a formal letter, you know how templates work. You start with a structure that is purposefully generic, then you personalize it.

That's the point of the Lord's Prayer. It's meant to be personalized, not copied-and-pasted verbatim into your prayer life.

Chances are, you've heard this prayer enough times to have some or all of it memorized. It even shows up in movies, often chanted by an overly solemn priest and a bored congregation, or recited by some poor soul facing an impending apocalypse. Hollywood loves its stereotypes.

However, the Lord's Prayer is anything but a boring chant or a prayer of resignation. It's actually a simple but revolutionary way to pray.

KEEP OUT OF THE GUTTER

Think of the Lord's Prayer as bumper bowling. If you've ever been bowling with little kids (or if you are terrible at bowling and don't care who knows it), you know what bumper bowling is.

Normal bowling involves rolling a ball down a long lane to knock over a triangle-shaped group of pins. We all know that. The problem is that on both sides of the lane, there is a gutter. If your aim is off, your ball ends up in the gutter and does a long, slow roll of shame into oblivion.

Hence, bumper bowling. Bumpers are placed in the gutters on both sides of the lane. Now, if your child (or you) can get the ball rolling in the right direction, it will eventually knock down some pins. It's not cheating—it's just bowling with a little help.

The Lord's Prayer is like having bumpers for prayer. It's praying with a little help. It gives you an outline to follow, some topics to cover, and even some language to use if you're unsure what to say. If you're intimidated by prayer and/or feel like your prayer times often end up in some cosmic gutter, following this model can help.

Let's look briefly at each phrase in this prayer. Again, prayer is not meant to be a ritual, so don't turn the Lord's Prayer into one. Notice Jesus begins by saying, "This is _how_ you should pray," not "This is _what_ you should pray." It's not an incantation. You don't unlock a heavenly level by getting the words right or nailing the intonation.

> **Prayer is not meant to be a ritual, so don't turn the Lord's Prayer into one.**

We humans have an amazing ability to take truths and turn them into formulas. Something about structure makes us feel safe, I guess. But if we exchange heart for structure, we're missing the point.

Prayer isn't "safe." (We'll talk more about that in the next chapter.) Prayer is raw and real, authentic and honest, unscripted and unrestrained. So as we look at this prayer, let your mind and spirit catch the heart of prayer, not just the structure of it.

The Lord's Prayer

Our Father in heaven,
hallowed be your name,
your kingdom come,
your will be done,
on earth as it is in heaven.
Give us today our daily bread.
And forgive us our debts,
as we also have forgiven our debtors.
And lead us not into temptation,
but deliver us from the evil one.

Matthew 6:9–13

Each of these lines teaches us something about how to pray. That was Jesus' purpose in giving it to us in the first place. So as we go through each line, don't just try to understand the meaning—practice it. Ask yourself, "How can I add this concept into my own prayer?"

Then do it.

Some days you might pray through the entire prayer, line by line, personalizing each topic. That's a fantastic way to learn to pray. Other days you might pick one and spend all your time there. Again, that's great.

However you use it, this simple prayer is a great way to begin learning to pray like Jesus did.

"OUR FATHER IN HEAVEN"

Jesus starts His prayer with a phrase that is simple and yet profound beyond anything we can fully grasp on earth: "Our Father in heaven." This tells us a lot about God.

He's not a force. He's a person.

He's not an impersonal being. He yearns for relationship with us.

He's not subject to the limitations of earth. He's the God of heaven.

He's not against us. He is for us.

He's our Father.

God created us, then He redeemed us. He adopted us as His kids. And there is nothing that can separate us from His love.

The God of all creation, the ruler of the universe, is our dad.

I've known that my whole life, but it took becoming a dad myself to really start to grasp the depth of this. I love my kids more than the world. Yes, I joke about the challenges of parenthood, but I wouldn't trade those challenges for any comfort, any convenience, any luxury. I love my kids. Period.

Even at five o'clock in the morning when no human being should be awake, and yet they are.

Even at 11 p.m. when I want some alone time with my wife, but they keep popping out of bed like characters in a Whac-A-Mole game.

Even when—especially when—they are sick or sad or scared, and they need someone to trust and hug.

They are mine, and nothing will ever change that.

That's how God feels about us. We don't come to God in prayer as our boss or our overlord or a judge waiting to decide whether to condemn or acquit us, but as His *children*. Sit with that for a few minutes and just think about it.

Inhale: I am God's child.

Exhale: I am safe in His presence.

Honestly, I think that if we grasped this simple truth, everything would change. How much worry, guilt, fear, and condemnation do we carry because we see God as something other than our Father?

The second part of this verse says, "hallowed be your name." To hallow something is to recognize it as holy. God's holiness is an integral part of who He is, and it is foundational to our relationship with Him. This reminds us of another simple truth we often forget: It's not about us.

Our prayers tend to come out of our needs and desires. That's natural, and there's nothing wrong with it. But it means our prayers are likely to be a bit us-centered.

One of the most important aspects of prayer is that it helps us reframe our lives. Our perspective shifts in prayer: from our weaknesses to His greatness, from our failures to His holiness, from our need to His supply, and from our goals to His purposes.

No matter what words you choose to pray, beginning with these two truths— God is our Father, and life isn't all about me—is a powerful way to start seeing reality as God does.

If you can, take a moment right now to make this personal. Meditate on what the truths in this first line mean for you and spend a few moments praying about them. That might look like telling God thank-you, asking Him to help you understand these truths, or something else entirely. It's up to you. There is no script.

Practicing the Lord's Prayer

Our Father in heaven

- What emotions come to mind when I pray to God as, "My Father"?
- How does He view me?
- What rights and benefits do I have as God's child?

Hallowed be your name

- How big and great and powerful is God to me?
- Have I made life too much about me?
- Where is my focus—on God or only on myself? Does He want to shift anything in my perspective?

"YOUR KINGDOM COME, YOUR WILL BE DONE"

The second line of the Lord's Prayer says, "your kingdom come, your will be done, on earth as it is in heaven."

This doesn't mean that God is not sovereign here on earth. Instead, it is a recognition of the current reality of sin, shame, disease, death, hatred, and a host of other things not found in heaven.

And in the midst of that chaos, we are asking God to be just as sovereign, just as powerful, just as triumphant, as if none of those things had any power.

Because they don't. Well, they do and they don't at the same time. On one hand, the pain and evil of this world have real consequences. We can't deny that, and prayer should embrace reality, not ignore it. But on the other hand, nothing we face in this life is bigger than God.

The "real reality" is that God is more powerful than our circumstances. That's the point of this line: recognizing the sovereignty of God. Before God, nothing stands. There is no failure, no weakness, no enemy, no problem that lies outside His power and authority.

So when we come to God in prayer, it is with a recognition that He has all we need.

Notice that up until now, the prayer has not even mentioned our needs, wants, or desires. "Our Father in heaven, hallowed be your name, your kingdom come, your will be done, on earth as it is in heaven." The prayer begins by recognizing who God is and surrendering our will to His.

Now, your prayers don't always have to start with this lofty, mature perspective. A lot of mine don't. They go more like this: "Dear Jesus . . . help!" And I'm in good company with that prayer. As we saw earlier, David sent up SOS prayers all the time. Just read the book of Psalms.

If you're not in a crisis moment, though, praying that God's will would be done before you pull out your list of needs is a good habit. It's a way of reminding ourselves that we are not the senior partner in this relationship, we aren't the experts on life, and our wish is not His command.

Letting God be God is a good thing. We would be terrible at that job.

Imagine if five-year-olds ruled the world for a day, and every idea they had was promptly carried out by adults. On the one hand, it could be the most entertaining thing ever. On the other, it wouldn't take long before the world descended into total chaos. School would be outlawed, sinks would flow with chocolate milk, and bedtime would simply not happen.

Kids need adults because they aren't the best judges of their own needs. And the difference in maturity and wisdom between a kindergartner and an adult is nothing compared to the difference between us and God. Praying that His will would be done reminds us that we aren't as smart as our Twitter bio or our résumé makes us sound.

Also, notice that the line doesn't say, "your will be done in my life, God, because it's my life that really matters here."

It says, "on earth."

Your problems and needs are real. And they are almost as important as mine are. Just kidding, of course. But that's how we tend to think, right? Our problems take precedence over those of others.

God, unsurprisingly, has a bigger perspective. And prayer has a way of helping us zoom out a bit and see the bigger picture.

It's amazing when you think about it. Jesus is asking us to partner with God in prayer, not just to get our own needs met but to see His kingdom—His power, love, glory, and purpose—accomplished on earth. That realization adds a whole new dimension to our prayers.

Practicing the Lord's Prayer

Your kingdom come, your will be done, on earth as it is in heaven.

- Am I committed to obeying God?
- Do I trust Him enough to do what He says?
- Specifically, what is God's will in my family today?
- What is His will in my work, school, or friendships?
- What is His will in the world around me, both locally and globally?

"GIVE US TODAY OUR DAILY BREAD"

The next line says, "Give us today our daily bread." But the ultimate meaning isn't bread (all the gluten-free folks can breathe a sigh of relief)—it's everything we need to survive. It's the essentials that God knows we have to have, such as food, water, clothing, shelter, and coffee. Definitely coffee.

There are several important truths packed into this short sentence.

First, it's bold. Jesus isn't telling us to come to God like strangers hoping for a favor, but as sons and daughters confident that He will meet our needs.

Because that's what dads do.

Second, it's honest. There's no beating around the bush, no pretending our needs don't exist or don't matter. God doesn't just tolerate your requests, He _asks_ for them. He expects them. So don't pretend you don't matter. You're a child of God, and He delights in meeting your needs.

Remember, pray about everything, and be anxious about nothing.

Be real. Be honest. Be specific. That doesn't obligate God to do everything you ask, of course. He can and does say "No," or "Wait," or even, "Are you kidding me right now?" But honesty is a mark of an authentic relationship, so don't be afraid of it.

Third, it's daily. It might seem more efficient to say, "God, could you please just take care of every single need I will ever have, every day, for the rest of my life? Thanks, bro. Talk to you in eternity," but that's not how prayer works.

Because it's not how relationship works.

It's not how God works either. God meets our needs daily. Very often, He doesn't meet any needs further ahead than that.

That might scare us. Not having security regarding the future can be frightening.

If we think about it a little more, though, we realize we have _complete_ security regarding the future. God's promises are faithful and true forever. He doesn't need to give us a year's supply of bread today. (What would we do with that much bread, anyway? Open a bakery? Overfeed ducks in the park?)

We can be confident that He will meet our needs: all of them, every day, for the rest of our lives.

Daily prayer for those needs draws us closer to God in a way nothing else does. It reminds us of our ongoing need for Him, and it helps us see how He meets our needs over and over.

What's on your "I need" list today? If you're like me, there are a lot. That's okay. But there are usually one or two that are triggering the most anxiety, confusion, or fear.

Start with those. Lean in to them. Share not just the needs, but your emotions when you think of those needs.

Come before Him confidently. I love this encouragement from the author of Hebrews: "Let us then approach God's throne of grace with confidence, so that we may receive mercy and may find grace to help us in our time of need" (4:16).

Pray about everything, be anxious about nothing. Nowhere is that more needed than in regard to the things you need today.

Practicing the Lord's Prayer

Give us today our daily bread.

- What is worrying me right now?
- What are my urgent physical or financial needs?
- What needs do I have in my family or friendships?
- Are there things I should be doing with regard to my needs, knowing that God is working on my behalf?

"FORGIVE US OUR DEBTS"

The next line says, "and forgive us our debts, as we also have forgiven our debtors." *Debts* doesn't literally mean money owed us. It means anything someone has done to hurt or offend us.

We talked about this earlier when we looked at prayers that are a waste of time. If we are full of bitterness or offense, God wants us to resolve that, not ignore it. Living in peace with our brothers and sisters is high on His priority list.

If we're honest with ourselves, we know that we need God's grace. We know where we've messed up, even if others don't. That's why we have the gospel.

The word _gospel_ literally means "good news," and the good news is that God does not hold our failures, sins, mistakes, or weaknesses against us. He's wiped the slate clean.

Of course, after God wipes that slate clean, we often scribble all over it again. We covet, or hate, or lust, or lie, or lose our tempers in traffic, or yell at the dog, or drink decaffeinated coffee, or whatever.

And God forgives that too. He doesn't hold it against us. He doesn't take a screenshot of our sin before deleting it just in case He needs to refer to it later. He forgives us.

Wonderful, right?

And then He asks us to treat others with that same love.

Ouch.

I'm a much happier recipient of forgiveness than I am a giver of it.

But God doesn't pull any punches in this area. He expects us to forgive those who sin against us. This isn't so they get off the hook. It isn't so they can continue to hurt others. It isn't because you don't matter, or because you deserved what they did to you. All of those ideas are completely false. (Again, see chapter 13. This topic is one that Christians sometimes get wrong, and that can lead to tolerating abusive situations.)

Forgiveness is defined by psychologists as a conscious choice to release feelings of resentment or vengeance toward someone who has hurt you, regardless of whether they deserve forgiveness.[1]

Forgiveness is for you. When you release the person who hurt you, you relinquish their control over your heart, your thoughts, your emotions, your present, and your future. You acknowledge the offense and the pain it caused, but you refuse to allow that to dictate the rest of your life.

There is freedom in forgiveness.

Who do you need to forgive? That's a tough question, and I can't answer it for you. It's one you need to ask yourself, though.

Right now, or when you next sit down to pray, pray this courageous prayer: "God, who do I need to forgive, and will you help me do that?"

Then sit and listen. Cry if you need to. Reach out for help if that feels appropriate. Trust your Father to help you walk the path of authentic forgiveness and find the freedom your heart yearns to have. Forgiveness is a gateway to deep joy and peace.

Practicing the Lord's Prayer

Forgive us our debts, as we also have forgiven our debtors.
- What people or circumstances have hurt me?
- Who do I need to forgive?
- Is forgiveness hard for me? If so, why?
- What do I need to find healing?

"LEAD US NOT INTO TEMPTATION"

The final line says, "And lead us not into temptation, but deliver us from the evil one."

Despite how the traditional English translation sounds, Jesus isn't suggesting that God tempts us to sin or causes us to fail. That wouldn't even make sense. Life is challenging enough for us already, without having God himself trying to trip us up. The apostle James makes sure we get this straight: "No one should say, 'God is tempting me.' For God cannot be tempted by evil, nor does he tempt anyone" (1:13).

While there are different opinions about the meaning of Jesus' words here, the gist of the line could be stated this way: "God, help me not fail when I am tested."[2]

We face challenging situations all the time. They might be caused by external forces, including difficult circumstances or even demonic influence. They might come from internal desires, including ones that are normal but need to be controlled, and others that are simply wrong. They test our character, faith, and determination.

Put another way, they tempt us.

They tempt us to act like people we don't want to be.

They tempt us to get what we want using the wrong means.

They tempt us to do things that at our core we don't want to do.

They tempt us to react in ways that don't align with our core values.

They tempt us to become something other than what God has made us to be.

Jesus said to pray about all that.

Jesus was honest. He didn't sugarcoat things. He made it clear that following Him would not always be easy, that temptations are real, that the "evil one" (a reference to the devil) will oppose us, and that faith in God doesn't make all our wrong desires magically disappear.

I wish it did. That would make me feel a lot better about myself. In fact, if I never struggled with temptation or sin, I might assume I was a pretty good guy, leading a pretty good life. I'd be proud of myself. I'd be arrogant. And I'd probably be a jerk.

Bill Gates once said, "Success is a lousy teacher. It seduces smart people into thinking they can't lose."[3]

If we are always the top of the class, the king of the mountain, the star of the show, we will likely end up stunted in our growth and puffed up in our egos. That's where our failures and struggles do us a favor, though. They bring us back to reality.

Personal limitations bring us to the end of ourselves, which is a good place to be. That is where grace begins.

There are days when problems seem to roll in like waves, one after the other, each taking their turn to tumble us in the surf. At those moments, when we're tempted to run from what God has called us to do, or take a shortcut that would compromise our integrity, or just curl up in a fetal position and try to survive, prayer is a lifeline.

Jesus knew His disciples would face all kinds of tests and trials. He knew most of them would give their lives for the gospel. He knew they'd feel like quitting at times.

He knows we feel that way too. And He gently calls us to bring those feelings to Him, in prayer.

God promises to help us in difficult times: "And God is faithful; he will not let you be tempted beyond what you can bear. But when you are tempted, he will also provide a way out so that you can endure it" (1 Corinthians 10:13).

God is for you. He wants you to succeed. And He's ready to help you do it: to live in the victory, joy, and peace that you were created to experience.

Practicing the Lord's Prayer

Lead us not into temptation, but deliver us from the evil one.
- What difficult situations am I facing right now?
- Am I strong in courage, integrity, and faith?

- How are my emotions and thoughts doing?
- Do I feel attacked? Am I responding the right way?
- Do I feel tempted in any area? Where do I need God's help to do what's right?

Whether you're new to prayer or just feel like there is more for you to discover, the Lord's Prayer is a practical, simple, and yet profound model to use.

I encourage you to try praying through this prayer, line by line. Take time to think through each concept, meditating on them and personalizing them.

Don't limit yourself to the ideas or questions in this chapter. Those are just my thoughts to get you started. To get the bowling ball rolling down the lane, so to speak. The more you use this prayer, the more you will see in it, and the more you will get out of it.

Two thousand years ago, the disciples asked Jesus, "Lord, teach us to pray."

He did. And He's still teaching us today.

SIXTEEN

These are dangerous prayers

In 1950, a brilliant, creative theologian named C.S. Lewis wrote a children's book called *The Lion, the Witch and the Wardrobe*, which was part of a larger series of books about the fictitious land of Narnia. You might have read the book, or—like me—maybe you watched the movie. Besides being a great story in its own right, this story is an allegory for many elements of the Christian faith.

At one point, the protagonists—four siblings: Lucy, Edmund, Susan, and Peter—meet a pair of talking Narnian beavers, rather predictably called Mr. and Mrs. Beaver. The children have heard rumors of the great king Aslan (who represents Jesus in the story) returning to make wrongs right and save Narnia from the evil White Witch.

The children ask Mr. Beaver about Aslan, and he gives them some startling news: Aslan isn't human at all. In His words:

> "Aslan is a lion—*the* Lion, the great Lion."

> "Ooh!" said Susan, "I'd thought he was a man. Is he—quite safe? I shall feel rather nervous about meeting a lion."

"That you will, dearie, and no mistake," said Mrs. Beaver. "If there's anyone who can appear before Aslan without their knees knocking, they're either braver than most or else just silly."

"Then he isn't safe?" said Lucy.

"Safe?" said Mr. Beaver. "Don't you hear what Mrs. Beaver tells you? Who said anything about safe? 'Course he isn't safe. But he's good. He's the King, I tell you."[1]

I love that thought: Jesus is good, but He's not "safe." That is, He's not tame. He isn't a pet. He can't be controlled or predicted or subdued.

Most pictures and paintings of Jesus show Him looking serene, even detached, posing passively for the artist with sad eyes and a halo around His head. (He's also usually white, blond, and blue-eyed, which is another fallacy.)

But the real Jesus didn't look like a Caucasian mystic on weed. Jesus was strong, active, and present. He was a blue-collar worker, comfortable hanging out with fishermen and laborers and people who were rough around the edges. He was blunt, edgy, even sarcastic at times. He made people laugh and He made them squirm. Jesus healed people, and raised the dead, and cast out demons. He brought heaven down to earth in such a real way that it scared people at times.

Yes, there is security in Jesus. He is a safe place in the sense of being strong, faithful, and trustworthy. But if your idea of safety is a god you can keep on a leash, then no, Jesus is not safe, any more than taking a lion on a walk would be.

And prayer isn't either.

In prayer, we interact with the untamed and untamable God who created the universe, who sent Jesus to die in our place, who can and does do miracles, who knows us better than we know ourselves, and who has absolutely no problem getting all up in our business.

In this chapter, I want to look at a few prayers that I call dangerous prayers. These are prayers such as commitment, surrender, dedication, repentance, transparency, and prayer for your enemies.

They are dangerous because they will take you places you might not have anticipated—but you won't regret them. Prayer isn't safe. But it is good.

1. NOT MY WILL, BUT YOURS.

Remember that iconic line in *The Princess Bride* that Wesley would repeat to the princess: "As you wish"?

The last time he said the phrase, it was more like, "AS YOU WIIIIIIIIIISH," because Wesley was shouting it while he tumbled down a hillside into the fire swamp. This was the climactic moment where the princess realized her true love had returned. And she had pushed him off a cliff.

True love hurts, apparently.

True love also surrenders itself to another. Not in a toxic, blind, codependent way, but in a faithful way. A covenant way. A trusting way. It says, "As you wish," as part of a mutual surrender.

God wants us to surrender to Him this way. Why? Because He's a despot? Some celestial tyrant bent on control?

No. Because He loves us, and we love Him. This is a mutual surrender, in a sense—God has already promised to be with us, to care for us, to listen to us, to respond to us. He has chosen to link himself to us, which is a crazy thought.

We are in a committed relationship, and if that relationship is going to survive fire swamps, rodents of unusual size, and the ups and downs of regular life, there needs to be trust.

Surrender means giving up control or ownership of something. If you have ever prayed the Lord's Prayer (in the last chapter, for example), then you've asked God, "Your will be done on earth as it is in heaven." That is surrender, at least in a general sense.

Surrender, however, needs to be a lot more personal than just a blanket prayer for an entire planet. It involves asking God to do His will in the practical, day-to-day decisions you make—finances, marriage, career, character, friendships. It is a surrender motivated by love and trust.

Jesus prayed this way. Remember the garden of Gethsemane, just before He went to the cross? "My Father, if it is possible, may this cup be taken from me. Yet not as I will, but as you will" (Matthew 26:39).

It's easy to think of Jesus as some emotionless deity who really didn't mind dying. After all, that's what He came for. And He knew in advance about the whole resurrection plot twist.

But Jesus was just as human as you or me. He felt physical sensations and had bodily weaknesses. He experienced emotions. And He knew what awaited Him when He was arrested.

Matthew records that three times on the night before He was arrested, He asked God not to send Him to die. But each time, He ended His prayer with a variation of, "Your will be done" (verses 39, 42, 43).

It's unlikely any of us will face the death penalty for obeying Jesus. Our struggles are real, but they at least don't involve crucifixion. This prayer is still just as relevant, though, and as powerful—and as difficult. We like to cling to our plans and our preferences, especially if we have a feeling that God's way is going to be painful.

This prayer is dangerous because it involves us consciously choosing to submit to God's plan even though we can see already that we aren't going to like it. At least not at first.

This prayer is all about trust. *All* prayer is about trust, I suppose, but this one even more so. This is when we put our money where our mouth is. This is where we choose His path even though we can see already that He's going a different direction than we would choose to go. That's the essence of trust.

Have you prayed this prayer? If not, are you ready to? It doesn't require eloquence, experience, or knowledge. Just your heart. A willingness to submit your plans to His and to follow His path even if it looks painful.

And there might be some pain. Pain is part of every journey. But doing things your way won't avoid pain either. God's way is something you will never regret in the end.

Chances are, you've prayed a prayer of surrender already. The day you decided to become a Christian, you said something like, "Jesus, I need you. I invite you to be my Lord and my Savior." You asked God to become the Lord—the boss, the head, the owner—of your life.

When we surrendered our lives to God, He didn't take control like a pilot operating a drone. We still retain our free will. God created us in His image, and part of that image is the ability to make choices.

But we did surrender. We turned ownership of our lives over to God. We became His.

Surrender, however, isn't a one-time thing. When we prayed that first prayer, we probably didn't understand all the ramifications of it. There were parts of our world we weren't ready to give to God, even if we didn't realize it.

God did, though. He accepted us anyway. And then, He got to work.

From that first prayer until now (and from now until the day we meet Him again in heaven), God is engaging in the art of gentle persuasion, revealing to us the areas we have yet to surrender to Him.

God cares about us and those around us. He knows that on our own, we won't always make the best decisions. We were created to be with God, to follow Him, to learn from Him. Not to be independent mini-gods trying to run our lives on our own.

How does God gently persuade us to yield our will to His? Often, He uses prayer. I can't tell you how many times I've come to God in prayer because I needed something, only to have Him point out some area of my life that wasn't nearly as surrendered as I'd thought.

When this happens, I instantly give the area to God in humility and maturity, and I move on, never to struggle again.

Yeah, right.

What I actually do, more often than not, is explain to God why He's wrong and why my bitterness or selfishness or anxiety is justified. Of course, I don't phrase it that way, but that's what I'm doing.

It never works. Sooner or later, God gets through to my heart and helps me see things His way.

Deep down, I want to do what's right, just like you do. I know that His way is going to be a lot better than mine. So even if my initial response is less than exemplary sometimes, I really do try to surrender my attitude or actions or plan to God.

I do that through prayer.

There is no formula to this prayer. The words aren't the key. Your heart is.

By the way, surrender doesn't mean you no longer have any responsibility in an area. You can't say, "I surrender my finances to God," and then whip out your credit card and start charging everything "to the Kingdom."

Nor does surrender mean you stop having emotions about what He's asking you to give up. In fact, surrendering is likely to stir up strong emotions indeed.

Surrender won't feel safe, but it's good for the soul.

It means that you consciously entrust yourself to God. Every emotion, every plan, every desire, every experience.

When was the last time you did this? Next time you pray, I encourage you to pray this type of prayer. Ask God, "Is there anything I have been clinging to instead of surrendering to you?"

This is a dangerous prayer. It demands that you give up control. None of us like that—but we all need it.

Surrender won't feel safe, but it's good for the soul.

2. I'M SORRY; PLEASE FORGIVE ME.

You might have heard that the three most important words in a relationship are, "I love you." You'd be wrong, though.

The three most important words are, "Let's get tacos." Nothing says love like tacos.

Well, almost nothing. There is one other phrase. It's not easy to say, but it may well have rescued more relationships than any other (including the offer of tacos).

"I am sorry."

If you've been in a relationship for longer than about three days, either you or the other person has probably done something that annoyed, frustrated, hurt, confused, or insulted the other one. We humans have an amazing ability to get under each other's skins.

Often our first response after we mess up is to protect ourselves. We hide what we have done, or we deny it, or we twist the story enough to make the other person think it's their fault, or we blame a third party, or whatever.

That might protect our egos, but it doesn't help our relationships. It's only when we are willing to own our faults, admit our failures, and say, "I am sorry" that true relationship flourishes.

This dynamic exists in our relationship with God as well. Do you want an intimate, open, trusting relationship with God? If so, honesty is vital. That is especially true when you've done something wrong.

That's why confession and repentance are so important.

Confession is admitting our faults and failures: "I did this. I said that. I went there. I responded this way. I made that decision." Confession is specific, personal, and honest.

Repentance takes this a step further; it means being willing to act differently going forward: "I want to change. I don't want to do that again. I am going to be better and do better."

You can't have one without the other in a healthy relationship. Admitting our faults and being willing to change are essential.

The wonderful thing is that unlike human relationships, we can confess our faults and sins to God without fear that He will reject us. He already knows what we've done, for one thing. He's already forgiven us, for another.

Our confession isn't to let God know what we've done. It's more for our own sake: to admit to ourselves before God that we have fallen short, and we need His mercy.

Earlier I quoted Hebrews 4:16: "Let us then approach God's throne of grace with confidence, so that we may receive mercy and may find grace to help us in our time of need." The phrase _throne of grace_ is indescribably comforting to me. God is the judge. His throne room is the courthouse, and His throne is the judgment seat of God. That's why it's so amazing that it's a throne of _grace_.

Not a throne of wrath.

Not a throne of punishment.

Not a throne of condemnation.

Not even a throne of exasperation or annoyance.

It's a throne of grace.

When I confess my sins, weaknesses, failures, or faults to God, His response is pure grace. That reaction of grace is what gives us confidence to approach Him. We know that His first reaction is not to chastise us, but to aid us.

Notice that the verse doesn't just describe a grace to put up with us and our failures, but rather a grace "to help us in our time of need."

Grace is more than God's patience. Grace is God's power actively working to strengthen us when we are at our weakest.

Is there anything you need to confess to God? Are you holding on to an attitude, a habit, or a plan that you know doesn't reflect who you are in Christ?

Bring it to God in prayer. You weren't meant to carry your weaknesses alone. It's a heavy burden, one that you don't want or need. Confess it to God. Ask for help. Expect His grace—He promised it, after all.

Then leave the past behind. God doesn't hold your past against you, so don't hold it against yourself.

Confession and repentance lead to grace, and grace gives us hope, and hope points to the future.

3. HERE I AM; SEND ME.

The prophet Isaiah once had a vision in which he heard God asking for someone willing to be His messenger to Israel. Isaiah's response was, "Here am I. Send me!" (Isaiah 6:8). God did send him, and Isaiah became one of the most well-known prophets in history.

That prayer, "Here am I, send me!" is dangerous. It's a rejection of a predictable, comfortable life in favor of an adventure into the unknown with God.

It's often used in the context of doing missions work overseas. But the prayer is much broader than that. Isaiah spent most of His life ministering to His own people and His own country, after all.

"Send me" isn't about geography. It's about *purpose*. You may not end up thousands of miles away from home, eating unidentifiable foods and urgently learning the word for *bathroom* in a foreign language. You may not even leave your community.

I would go so far as to say that if you can't serve your local community, you don't have any business crossing the world. Performative missions, charity photo-ops, and savior complexes are not how the world is going to see Jesus.

They will see Jesus in your love.

Start by loving those close to you, by letting God send you to your neighbor and co-worker and friend. Maybe He'll send you to another nation, maybe not.

But He will send you. Of that you can be sure.

When you ask God to send you, you are praying to be used by Him to show His love to others. The prayer isn't about tasks as much as about people. God's purpose is always tied to people.

That doesn't mean you have to have a particular personality type. You might love meeting people, being in social situations, and interacting with others. Or you might be someone who wishes your plus-one at social events could be your cat.

God created both extremes and everything in between. He made you, and He wants to send you. You have something to offer others: your personality, your gifts, your experiences, your wisdom, your perspective, your voice. And most of all, your love.

Letting God "send" you doesn't mean you will never fail. You will fail at times. We all do.

You have to believe that your contribution outweighs your mistakes. Obviously you should avoid as many mistakes as possible and learn from the ones you do make. I'm not justifying incompetence here.

But I think we struggle less with *competence* and more with *confidence*.

You have to know your value to the team. And if you're ever in doubt about that, go to God, the greatest coach of all, and let Him give you a locker room pep talk.

Kobe Bryant was one of the greatest basketball players to ever live, and he's a personal hero of mine. He is famous for making a ridiculous number of points per game—and for missing a ridiculous number of shots. He currently ranks #4 in NBA history for career points scored[2] and #1 in shots missed.[3]

Do you know how he kept taking shots, even with so many misses? He had an unshakable commitment to self-confidence. He didn't just know he was good; he knew he needed to keep reminding himself that he was good.

Sports Illustrated contributor Chris Ballard highlights Kobe's mentality about self-confidence by recounting a conversation Kobe and filmmaker Gotham Chopra had after they watched a basketball game together. Here is his description of that exchange.

> Recalls Chopra, "Deron Williams went like 0-for-9. I was like, 'Can you believe Deron Williams went 0-9?' Kobe was like, 'I would go 0-30 before I would go 0-9. 0-9 means you beat yourself, you psyched yourself out of the game, because Deron Williams can get more shots in the game. The only reason is because you've just now lost confidence in yourself.'"[4]

I don't think Kobe was trying to throw shade; he was just pointing out that any player who stopped at nine shots had already given up. For Kobe, missing shots wasn't failure—but not taking shots certainly was.

Even hockey star Wayne Gretzky is quoted as saying, "You miss 100% of the shots you don't take."

Whether it's a team you coach, a mom's group you join, an immigrant community you volunteer in, or a nation you move to, there are people around you who need what you bring to the game.

I challenge you to pray this prayer, if you are ready: "Here am I, Lord, send me." Or, if you're more of a sports person, go with, "Here am I, Coach, put me in the game."

You have shots to take.

Points to score.

People to help.

A world to love.

It's time get in the game.

4. SEARCH MY HEART.

Another prayer that may lead you places you wouldn't have expected is this one: "Search my heart."

This is an invitation for God to probe your innermost being: your thoughts, your motives, the deepest secrets of your heart.

The things you don't want anyone to know about.

The fears you haven't admitted to yourself.

The hopes buried deep in your heart.

The dreams you don't think could ever come to pass.

God doesn't need your permission, of course. He sees it all anyway. That's why David wrote, "You have searched me, LORD, and you know me. You know when I sit and when I rise; you perceive my thoughts from afar" (Psalm 139:1–2).

But the same David wrote,

> Search me, God, and know my heart;
> test me and know my anxious thoughts.
> See if there is any offensive way in me,
> and lead me in the way everlasting.
>
> Psalm 139:23–24

We don't pray to give God permission to speak, but rather to acknowledge that we are listening.

We need to verbalize the desire for God to know us deeply, authentically, completely. We need to hear ourselves say it. It helps us be ready to respond when He speaks.

Because while God won't be surprised at what He finds in our hearts, we might be.

God spoke through Jeremiah, a prophet who spent years trying to get his countrymen to open their eyes to the sin that was destroying them, saying, "The heart is deceitful above all things and beyond cure. Who can understand it?" (Jeremiah 17:9).

In other words, the human heart is surprisingly good at self-deception. We think we know ourselves intimately, but we often don't even know how much we don't know about ourselves.

God answered His own question through Jeremiah: "I the LORD search the heart and examine the mind" (17:10). God sees past the external and gets straight to the heart: our heart.

Again, this is not an easy prayer—but it is liberating. Jesus was the one who said, "You will know the truth, and the truth will set you free" (John 8:32).

The truth hurts, and it triggers emotions we might not enjoy, but it leads to freedom, which is far more valuable.

I encourage you to set aside some time when you pray this. If you are the type who likes writing things down, make sure you have a notebook with you. If you prefer audio notes or something else, that's great. Find what works for you.

> **The truth hurts, and it triggers emotions we might not enjoy, but it leads to freedom, which is far more valuable.**

Then, in your own words, ask God to search you and tell you what He sees. Here are a few ways you could ask this, but feel free to add your own. After you pray each question, stop and listen. Don't rush. Give God the opportunity to whisper His answer.

"Dear God, search my heart. I give you access to every part of me."

"How do you feel about me?"

"What about me do you love?"

"What hopes or dreams have you put in my heart?"

"Are any of my actions, assumptions, or attitudes blocking my ability to hear your voice or obey?"

"What do you want to say to me today?"

If it helps you, write down what you feel He might be saying. Don't worry about grammar or spelling or eloquence. This isn't for anyone but you.

Just listen and be set free.

5. FORGIVE AND BLESS MY ENEMIES.

Jesus was born into a nation of people under the oppressive thumb of the Roman empire. They longed for the day when the Messiah would come to destroy their enemy and set them free. They assumed He would be a military hero who would lead them to battlefield victories and restore the glory of the kingdom of Israel.

Jesus, however, came with a different goal. He preached an upside-down kingdom where living comes from dying, giving is better than receiving, and "losing" brings victory.[5]

He had no interest in taking down an army. He was after the power of sin itself.

His messages fascinated His listeners. The poor and weak and downtrodden cheered. The powerful gritted their teeth.

Jesus, as usual, was after people's hearts. They didn't need a general; they needed a Savior.

During one of His most famous sermons, often called the Sermon on the Mount, Jesus made a statement that would have shocked every single person listening. It's no less shocking today.

> You have heard that it was said, "Love your neighbor and hate your enemy." But I tell you, love your enemies and pray for those who persecute you, that you may be children of your Father in heaven. He causes his sun to rise on the evil and the good, and sends rain on the righteous and the unrighteous.
>
> Matthew 5:43–45

The people had hoped to hear how God was going to destroy Israel's enemies. Instead, they were told to love them. To *pray* for them. And not the kind of prayer that goes, "Dear God, please kill my enemies," either.

Jesus wanted them to actually love their enemies. Because that's what God does.

Do you want to be like God? Do you want to act like your Father in heaven? Love your enemies. Forgive them. Bless them.

Most of us won't spend any time on a battlefield. We don't have people who are plotting our literal death. Hopefully, anyway.

But we do have enemies—people who oppose, hurt, or abuse us. The co-worker who stole credit for your work or sabotaged a promotion. The boss who used his power to manipulate or hurt you. The estranged friends who tried to ruin your reputation. The business partner who stole from you. The family member who abused you when you were a child.

This prayer may be the most difficult prayer in this chapter. It also may be the truest test of how well we are learning to live like Christ. After all, He lived this. On the cross, dying in agony, His only words regarding those who had hurt Him were a prayer: "Father, forgive them, for they do not know what they are doing" (Luke 23:34).

Jesus is asking us to take forgiveness all the way to the extreme of actively seeking the good of those who have hurt us.

At this point you're probably saying, "That's not fair!" No, it's not. That's the point. God doesn't treat us fairly, or we'd all be dead. His treatment of us isn't based on our actions but on His character.

That's what He is calling us to do as well.

Easy? No. Fun? Not really. But it is one of the most liberating things you will ever do.

We looked at the topic of forgiveness earlier, when we talked about bitter prayers and other ineffective ways of praying. Please don't misunderstand me—I don't believe that forgiving your enemies means pretending they are your friends or ignoring the harm they have done. It doesn't mean burying your trauma or silencing your voice. That is toxic forgiveness, and it doesn't do anybody any good.

But you can turn your enemies over to God. That's what Jesus did: He recognized that the ultimate judge was God. He didn't have to carry the burden of judging them or punishing them.

Paul encourages the Roman believers not to get even with their enemies because the Bible says, "'It is mine to avenge; I will repay,' says the Lord" (Romans 12:19). Since God will handle the revenge part, Paul continues, "'If your enemy is hungry, feed him; if he is thirsty, give him something to drink. In doing this, you will heap burning coals on his head.' Do not be overcome by evil, but overcome evil with good" (Romans 12:20–21).

Can you think of anyone who might qualify as an enemy? When you think of them, what emotions come to mind? Are you willing to bring those emotions, and the memories, to God?

It can help to pray some of the prayers earlier in this chapter (and even aspects of the Lord's Prayer) first. Our human way of thinking prefers revenge, not mercy, for those who have hurt us. It might take some time talking with God and listening to His perspective before you can honestly pray for those who have hurt you.

But when you do, it is freeing. Prayer is supernatural. Praying as Jesus did— that God would forgive and bless your enemies—can unleash healing and joy and peace in you. And who knows? It might just transform an enemy into a friend.

_____

All of these prayers—not my will, I'm sorry, send me, search my heart, and bless my enemies—are dangerous. They feel risky. Not risky in the sense that something bad might happen, but in the sense that you are giving up control, or at least the illusion of control.

These prayers push you out of the boat and onto the water with Jesus. They ask you to commit to God's ways and to live as Jesus did. They invite you to peel back the superficial layers of religion and surrender yourself—heart, soul, mind, and strength—to God.

Yes, they are scary and unpredictable.

But they are also liberating.

And life-transforming.

And releasing.

And healing.

And loving.

And brave.

Are you ready?

SEVENTEEN

What's on the menu?

I recently did some scholarly research on the topic of talking. And by research, I mean I typed "How to talk to . . ." into Google and looked at the top five autofill suggestions it gave me.

Here were Google's suggestions:

"How to talk to anyone"
"How to talk to girls"
"How to talk to someone at the IRS"
"How to talk to girls at parties"
"How to talk to Siri on Android"

Apparently, Google has concluded that I have no friends and no wife, owe back taxes, and cheat on Siri. So much for artificial intelligence.

Those are the first results my search engine served up to me, so they must be valuable to a lot of people. But there is one they missed that ought to be in anyone's top five: How to talk to God.

In one sense, of course, that's easy. We all know how to talk. But we also know that different scenarios call for different ways of talking. (Hence the Google results for negotiating with tax auditors versus flirting at a party. Those are very different art forms.)

Talking itself is one of many ways to communicate. All married couples know that verbal exchanges are about 1 percent of conjugal communication, because your spouse can read your eyes, your face, your mind, and your very soul. It's slightly terrifying.

So if human communication is so colorful and varied, why do we assume prayer is flat and one-dimensional? I've met people who think that prayer is talking to God on your knees by your bed at night. Period. Or you only talk to God during a specific thirty-second chunk of a church service when the pastor is leading the congregation.

That couldn't be further from the truth. Like any relationship, there are countless creative ways to pray.

If prayer were a restaurant menu, it wouldn't be In-N-Out. It would be the Cheesecake Factory. I'm not knocking In-N-Out. They keep it simple on purpose, and they do a good job. But Cheesecake Factory? Seriously, there are thirty-four choices just on the _cheesecake_ portion of the menu. I didn't even know that was possible.

I'm pretty sure heaven has a Cheesecake Factory.

There are more ways to pray than you might think.

Like cheesecake, there are more ways to pray than you might think. Different personalities, situations, or needs call for different approaches to prayer. In the following pages, we're going to explore a few of these approaches. This isn't an exhaustive list, but it's enough to get you started.

Think of this like a menu for prayer. I've grouped the items into categories for convenience, but you can use them however you wish. Pick whatever sounds good. Mix it up. Try something new. Find your favorites, then customize them. It's up to you.

SPEAKING

Speaking is the most obvious way to pray, but it includes a lot more than just saying words. Here are some ways you can pray that relate to speaking.

- *Praying silently* is easy, convenient, and probably the most common way people pray when they are praying alone.
- *Praying out loud,* even when you are alone, helps you to focus your thoughts so your mind doesn't wander. It also helps you remember what you are praying for during the rest of the day. Reading and thinking out loud have both been shown to help cognition and memory.[1]
- *Singing* is a great way to express yourself verbally and emotionally. You can sing worship songs, Scripture verses, or just your own words to any melody you like. No singing ability required.
- *Yelling, crying, groaning, sighing,* and *laughing* can also be legitimate ways to pray, especially during times of great pain or joy (Psalm 38:8–9; 56:8; 98:4). These are found throughout the Bible. Sometimes the most heartfelt prayers don't consist of intelligible words at all.
- *Praying in the Spirit,* also known as praying in tongues, builds up your spirit and soul (1 Corinthians 14:4).
- *Listening* is a part of any healthy relationship. Don't get so focused on saying what is in your heart that you forget to listen for God's reply. We'll look at this more in the next chapter, but for now, just be aware that prayer is more of a two-way conversation than we sometimes think it is.

READING AND WRITING

- *Reading prayers* that have been composed by others can be helpful if you don't know what to pray or if you just want to expand what you pray about. The Lord's Prayer is one example, but there are count-less others. Christians in many churches use written prayers as part of their corporate services and private devotional times.

- *Prayer cards or templates*, such as the one we use at Zoe Church (included at the end of this book), are useful, especially if you have a daily time of prayer and want to pray for a number of things.

- *Writing down your own prayers* helps you focus your thoughts, process and articulate what you are feeling, and remember what you have prayed. It also provides a written record you can go back to later. Often after God answers our prayers, we promptly forget about them. Going back occasionally to read through our prayers from the past can be a powerful reminder of how faithful He has been to meet our needs.

- *Journaling* involves writing not just your prayers but what you hear God saying to you, what you are feeling or thinking, or anything else that comes to mind. It has similar benefits as writing your prayers. Your journal can be handwritten, typed, or recorded as audio notes. Hey, you could even create a contact in your phone called "God" and text your thoughts to Him.

MOVEMENT

The following ways to pray have more to do with your posture or location than the words you say. Sitting in your favorite chair with a Bible and a weighted blanket might be the ideal way to pray for some people, but for others, that's just a clever way of saying "nap." Regardless of your personality, try adding movement to your prayer times and see what happens. Remember, we are wholistic beings. Our bodies and brains are linked in ways we don't often realize. Involving ourselves physically in prayer is natural and delightful.

- *Walking or pacing* while praying helps with alertness and burns a few calories at the same time. If you're the fidgety type, it also helps direct your energy so that it doesn't distract you.

- *Kneeling, lying down, or raising your hands* in prayer can be surprisingly powerful postures. When you feel in awe of God or sense a deep hunger to understand His sovereignty and power, try kneeling, lying prostrate, or raising your hands.
- *Hiking or camping* in the silence and beauty of God's creation are life-giving, soul-healing ways to commune with God. Go outside the city at night and find somewhere you can see the stars, then just meditate on God: His power, beauty, faithfulness, and love for His creation (which includes you).
- *Going for a walk or a drive* is a creative way to expand your prayers. Pray as you travel—for yourself, your neighborhood, your town. For the neighbor you see on the street. For the homeless person on the corner. For the passing strangers who are facing their own share of fears. For the guy who just cut you off, because that's what Jesus would do. For your world.

CREATIVITY

Many people express themselves better through art or through building something than they do through conversational speaking. If that's you, try using your art and your talents to communicate with God.

- *Write a poem.* Poetry uses form and rhythm to communicate more than what words alone can say. Psalms and other sections of the Bible are poetry, and they still resonate with us thousands of years later.
- Pray with your *music.* If you are musical, you may naturally reach for your guitar or sit down at a keyboard when you pray. Write a song or play one you know, or just play music without words, and offer that to God. He hears the wordless song of your spirit.
- *Draw or paint.* Art can be a way of communicating emotions, dreams, and desires that run deeper than words. It is also therapeutic, and when combined with prayer, can be a powerful way of bringing deep emotion to the surface and processing it with God.

- *Build or make something* as an act of worship. In medieval times, people used their resources and skills to build breathtaking cathedrals. It was their expression of faith, their means to glorify God.[2] You might find that crafting or building something is a way for you to feel closer to God.

CONTEMPLATION

Life for most of us is incredibly active, busy, and noisy. Social media and streaming services have only added to the temptation to fill every waking moment with *something*. Silence is rare. In fact, sometimes it seems like we avoid it, as if its presence makes us uncomfortable. But silence is a gift if we embrace it. Stillness is a treasure if we are willing to experience it. Sometimes, not doing anything is the most valuable thing we can do.

- *Meditation* is an ancient practice. Thanks to movies and TV shows, the word often conjures up images of yoga poses or exotic monks. The biblical concept of meditation is a bit different. Meditation in the Bible means contemplating or reflecting on God's Word (Joshua 1:8; Psalm 1:2–3). One way to do this is called *lectio divina*. It dates to the early centuries of Christianity and is still widely used today.[3] It's simple to do. Choose a passage of Scripture and read it slowly, line by line. The goal isn't to dissect its meaning so much as to receive what God wants to say to you through it. This isn't traditional Bible study; it's prayer. Take your time as you read. Listen. If a word or phrase stands out to you, stop and pray about it. Don't hurry. Don't be quick to move on. Meditate on that word or phrase for longer than you would usually do. See what comes to mind. Journal it if you wish. Then throughout your day, remind yourself of the word or phrase that came to you while reading.
- *Silence* is another way to commune with God. Psalm 46:10 says, "Be still and know that I am God." Rather than filling your whole prayer time with words, set aside time to just be still. It's surprisingly difficult. You might need to start with just one minute of silence, then

work your way up as you get better at the discipline. Quiet your mind, don't speak, and if your thoughts take over, bring them back to stillness. If you must focus on something, choose one attribute of God, and think about that. But don't try to explore the attribute or analyze it. Be still and sit with it for a while. Learn to find and value the joy of just being in God's presence, without an agenda or a time limit.

COMMUNITY PRAYER

Praying alone is a beautiful, intimate way to communicate with God, but praying in a group is valuable as well. It has a dynamic all its own. Faith and religion naturally create community, and that community is centered on a shared relationship with God. Praying together is a powerful way to express our faith and grow closer to one another. There is incredible power, encouragement, and life in praying with others.

- Pray with *one or two others*. Jesus said, "Where two or three gather in my name, there am I with them" (Matthew 18:20). You could meet with a friend, your spouse, a sibling—anyone willing to join you in prayer. It could be daily, weekly, monthly, or whenever you feel the need pray.
- Pray as part of a *small group*. This could be a formal group that meets regularly or an impromptu gathering of friends. It provides an opportunity to hear others' needs, to pray for and with them, and to be prayed for yourself. Not only is the prayer useful, but the fellowship, support, and counsel we are able to share with one another are life-giving.
- In church, *corporate* prayer will likely be part of the service. There may be time for everyone to pray at once out loud, or for corporate silent prayer, or for repeating written prayers in unison. All of these have value if they are from your heart. Participate as much as you are comfortable, and ask God to meet you where you are. Don't

compare yourself to others, but instead simply enjoy being in a community with people who share your faith.

- *Intercede* for others. *Intercession* is a term that refers to praying for other people. You might intercede alone or with other people, maybe for a few minutes or maybe much longer than that. Through intercessory prayer, you can help people and influence situations by going to God and asking for His grace and intervention on behalf of others.

More than likely, you have used at least one or two of these approaches to prayer. I encourage you to try a few others, even the ones you think are outside your comfort zone. Or maybe *especially* those.

Many of us are good at finding what works for us and turning that into a ritual or routine. The problem is that this habitual approach, this tendency toward spiritual routine, eventually undermines real relationship. It takes deliberate effort to stay out of ruts and to maintain a freshness of communion with God.

Think about the relationship you have with your closest friend—it is probably spontaneous and varied, right? You might see each other regularly and have certain traditions or routines, but you also have the freedom and closeness to relate in many other ways. You don't go into every conversation with a plan or a list of requests. You just hang out. You have fun together. You laugh, you cry, you rant, you vent, you listen, you learn, you grow.

Don't let yourself fall into empty rituals or spiritual boredom.

The same principle—that relationships need to be fresh, creative, exciting—is seen in healthy marriages. If you are married, you have probably discovered how valuable it is to explore new ways to connect and grow close. That can be a challenge, especially if there are small children running around everywhere. I speak from experience. But keeping things vibrant and exciting is absolutely vital to the health of your marriage.

If spontaneity and creativity bring life to friendship, marriage, and other human relationships, how much more will they enrich our walk with God? Don't let yourself fall into empty rituals or spiritual boredom.

Don't order the same thing off the menu every time, whether we're talking about cheesecake or prayer.

Experiment.

Pick something new.

Try something you've never done.

It might become your new favorite thing.

EIGHTEEN

The lost art of listening

We've covered a lot of territory in this book. I hope you are more excited about prayer than ever, and more confident that prayer is a skill you can excel at. In this final chapter, we are going to look at one of the topics of prayer that causes the most confusion and frustration: Learning to hear the voice of God.

Talking to God is easy, but listening to Him? Hearing His voice? Understanding His leading? That's a lot harder.

Speaking of talking, I do a lot of it. It's pretty much built into the job description of a preacher, after all. I literally get paid to stand in front of people and talk. There's a lot more to the job than that, of course, but that's the most public part.

Now, if you've been to very many church services, you know how this typically works—the preacher stands up front with a microphone, shares whatever is on their heart for longer than they meant to, apologizes for going overtime, keeps preaching, apologizes again, keeps preaching some more, prays a prayer that includes the points they didn't get to during their message, and finally closes the service.

I love it. I don't take it for granted at all. I'm aware that I'm sharing my own point of view, that I don't have all the answers, and that everybody listening to me has total freedom to agree or disagree with what I say. That's part of the fun.

I do have one pet peeve with preaching, though. What I'm about to describe doesn't happen every week, but when it does, it's usually the same people who do it.

After the closing prayer, while everybody is packing up their stuff and deciding where to eat lunch, someone will come up to me and say how much they loved the message, how much they agree with it, and how it's exactly what they've been thinking during the week. Then they'll spend ten minutes summarizing the sermon I just preached and sharing their favorite parts.

Except nothing they say will be what I said during the message. Nothing. At all.

It's like they're preaching their own sermon to an audience of one—yours truly. Maybe it's cosmic payback for the times I've been that guy preaching too long. I'm so glad they are engaged and excited, but they clearly weren't listening.

Here's the thing, though. I wonder how often I've done that to God? I show up in prayer with an agenda, a prayer list, and a plan. I tell God what He's thinking. I tell Him what He should do. I impose my ideas on Him. Then I walk away, happy to have expressed my point of view.

And God is like, "Bro, you haven't heard a thing I've been saying."

Prayer is not just a time for us to talk to God. It's also a time to listen to Him. To know Him better. To understand His ways. To gain His perspective.

If you look back over the benefits of prayer that we covered in the first section, you'll realize that the majority of prayer is not about us telling God stuff, but about us receiving something from Him. God wants to *communicate* with us. He wants us to hear His voice and His heart.

The Bible records over two thousand instances in the Old Testament alone when God spoke to people. In the New Testament, not only did God continue speaking, but He also promised to send the Holy Spirit to teach us and to remind us of what Jesus had said (John 14:26).

God wants to speak to us. In fact, He probably is doing so already, whether we realize it or not.

> **God wants to speak to us. In fact, He probably is doing so already, whether we realize it or not.**

When I discuss this topic with people, I hear one sentence (or some variation of it) over and over: "I don't know how to hear God's voice."

The emotions packed into that sentence range from frustration to confusion to shame. Most people assume that it ought to be easy (just like they assume prayer ought to be easy). And when it's not, they don't know what to do.

Is it their fault? God's fault? Some sixth sense they lack or a cosmic code they have yet to crack?

I think part of the issue is the wording we use. *Voice* and *hearing* imply our physical sense of hearing. But God very rarely speaks in audible form. He did that a few times in the Bible, and it scared the crud out of people.

I'm not suggesting we need different words. I don't think there are any. *Hearing* is as close as we can come to capturing what happens. And it is the term the Bible uses repeatedly.

Rather than changing the word, we need to expand it.

Hearing God doesn't happen with our ears, but with our hearts.

His voice doesn't vibrate in our eardrums; it resonates in our spirits.

It doesn't come as a hurricane, but as a gentle breeze.

It's easy to miss. It's easy to ignore (at least for a while).

But it's life-giving when we hear it.

Like any relationship, your interactions with God will be personal and unique, and will grow and develop at their own pace. I can't teach you techniques that will suddenly make God's voice easy to hear. Instead, I just want to share a few things that have helped me.

Learn from them if they're helpful, but don't follow them like a rule book.

Rather, come to God with the most precious gift you have to offer, and the only one He wants: yourself. Ground your prayer in God's promise: "You will seek me and find me when you seek me with all your heart" (Jeremiah 29:13). Meditate on what Jesus said in John 10:27, "My sheep listen to my voice; I know them, and they follow me."

We're humans. We don't always get spiritual things right. God doesn't expect us to. He is patient, kind, and loving. He meets us where we are.

But He doesn't leave us there; He draws us closer to Him and teaches us to hear Him better. And while that process is slow and can be difficult, it is immensely rewarding.

Seek Him. Listen for Him. Be patient, persevere, and trust that He will help you. You will learn to hear His voice.

HOW DO I KNOW IT'S GOD?

Before we look at practical ways to hear from God, let's talk about what God's voice sounds like.

How do we know if we are hearing from God or from our own desires? What is the difference between His thoughts and our thoughts? Did last night's dream come from God or the gluten we ate?

When it comes to hearing God's voice, I think the challenge often isn't so much hearing God's voice as it is picking that voice out from the chaos of other voices that clamor for our attention. There are simply so many things clamoring for our attention that it's hard to know which come from God and which don't.

Have you ever been at an airport gate or in some other crowded place, and somebody was watching videos on their phone . . . at full volume . . . without headphones? Meanwhile, everyone else is giving them passive-aggressive glances and wondering why they don't have more self-awareness. I always wish I had extra headphones to give them so I could graciously enable their video consumption while protecting the sanity of the rest of us.

What is fascinating, though, is how intently these headphonesless video watchers pay attention to the screen. They are surrounded by movement and noise and glares, but they are oblivious. They are tuned in to only one voice, one source of information.

Now, the video that holds their rapt attention is probably a cat skydiving, or a gender reveal party gone wrong, or a potato that looks like the Eiffel Tower. But to them, it's all that matters right then.

I want that same laser focus when it comes to listening to God. He's got a lot more to add to my life than goofy TikTok videos, after all. In a world full of noise and movement and stress and adrenaline, I want to be able to tune it all out when necessary, and just be with Jesus. I want to be able to pick His voice out from the cacophony around me.

So how do you know whether what you are hearing is from God? Here are a few suggestions.

1. God's voice agrees with His Word.

God never contradicts His written Word, the Bible.

What we think we are hearing Him say—in our hearts, through circumstances, from advice we receive, or any other way—is always subjective. That is, there's an element of doubt in it because we are fallible humans.

It might be true. But it might be false. Or, as is often the case, it might be a mixture of the two.

The Bible, on the other hand, is completely accurate. We don't have to worry about whether it's right or wrong. It might be a challenge to understand or to obey at times, but it's trustworthy.

That means we can and must compare what we think we hear with His Word. If it matches, then we have greater confidence that we are hearing correctly. If it doesn't, then we need to let it go.

It doesn't matter how many people, signs, dreams, or voices tell you that you can cheat on your taxes, cheat on your spouse, or slash your cranky neighbor's tires—that's not God.

He won't lead you to do something that contradicts His will and His character revealed in the Bible.

2. God's voice brings peace.

Sometimes that's an immediate peace: a stillness, calmness, sense of well-being. Other times it pushes us toward something difficult—such as apologizing to a person we've hurt—that brings peace once we've obeyed.

If the voice you're hearing leads to real peace, it's likely from God. If it brings confusion and chaos, it probably isn't Him at all. The Bible calls God "The Lord of peace," and peace should be a hallmark of our relationship with Him (2 Thessalonians 3:16; 1 Corinthians 14:33).

If you are evaluating different options in a particular decision, ask yourself: *What brings me the most peace? What decision will produce God's peace in the long run?*

3. God's voice is usually quiet.

It's easy to miss if you're not listening.

That means we need to be intentional about listening to God. Quieting our lives. Pausing our schedule regularly. Even slowing down our "normal" so that there are spaces built into every day to be still and listen.

God made this point to the prophet Elijah in dramatic fashion in 1 Kings 19:11–13. Elijah had just won a spectacular victory against the idolatrous Baal-worship that Israel was captivated by and had earned the enmity of the queen as a result. Her threats scared him so badly that he fled into the wilderness. He was exhausted, distressed, and scared, and he was desperate to hear from God.

So God responded. Look at how He made himself known to Elijah.

> The LORD said, "Go out and stand on the mountain in the presence of the LORD, for the LORD is about to pass by."
>
> Then a great and powerful wind tore the mountains apart and shattered the rocks before the LORD, but the LORD was not in the wind. After the wind there was an earthquake, but the LORD was not in the earthquake. After the earthquake came a fire, but the LORD was not in the fire. And after the fire came a gentle whisper. When Elijah heard it, he pulled his cloak over his face and went out and stood at the mouth of the cave.
>
> Then a voice said to him, "What are you doing here, Elijah?"

Elijah knew God's presence. It wasn't in the hurricane or the earthquake or the fire, although God was powerful enough to control those. God's presence was in the whisper. In the quietness. In the silence.

We need to make space in our lives to hear that whisper. Many people do this by having a time of devotions in the morning before they jump into the busyness of the day. Others prefer to do it at night, when the day is over and there is time to pause and reflect. Do what works for you in your current schedule and change it up if your schedule is adjusted.

4. God's voice is lovingly uncomfortable.

If God's voice conveniently agrees with your own thoughts all the time, it's probably not God. Read that again.

God speaks for himself. He confronts sin, reveals weaknesses, uncovers vulnerabilities, cleans out the wounds we've been trying to hide. He loves us enough to hurt us, but always for our good. He is the friend described in Proverbs 27:6: "Wounds from a friend can be trusted, but an enemy multiplies kisses."

God doesn't condemn, but He does convict.

Condemnation says, "You just did that wrong, and you did it that way because you are a failure. You do everything wrong, actually. You are terrible. You are worthless. You are hopeless." Condemnation writes us off as lost causes. It is general, vague, and permeated with despair and shame.

Conviction, on the other hand, brings hope. It says, "You did wrong, but I love you and have forgiven you already. Now you need to make it right, and you need to do things differently in the future." Conviction tells us that God loves us enough to correct us when we need it. It is specific, practical, and loving. And it comes with the grace to change.

I'm not saying God will always say things you hate to hear. He's not a divine critic who exists solely to point out your failures. Often, especially when you are weak or hurting, His voice will be both what you want and what you need. It will comfort and encourage, strengthen and support.

Whatever He says, it will be honest. It may not be what we expect to hear, hope to hear, or try to hear, but it will be what we need to hear. And it will bring healing and life.

Some of us have an internal critic who mercilessly critiques everything we do. That isn't God. Some of us have an internal fan club that tells us we are the greatest thing since avocado toast. That isn't God either. Both of those are likely reflections of our own self-image.

I remember another old preacher saying, "God comes to comfort the afflicted and to afflict the comfortable." That sounds about right.

God's voice will often say what you don't expect. It will reassure you but challenge you. It will give you inner peace but propel you outside your comfort zone. It will pat you on the back and kick your butt at the same time.

In a good way.

5. God's voice is considerate and loving toward others.

James gives us a useful description of God's voice when he says, "But the wisdom that comes from heaven is first of all pure; then peace-loving, considerate, submissive, full of mercy and good fruit, impartial and sincere" (3:17). Notice how many of those words relate to our social behavior: considerate, submissive, full of mercy, impartial, sincere.

God cares about how we treat people. He loves them just as much as He loves us. When we pray, we need to filter what we hear through the list above.

If my words start with "God told me . . ." and are followed by my demanding my rights, that's a red flag. Not that I don't have rights. I do. But I rarely need God to remind me of them. More often, I need Him to remind me that the way of the cross is one of sacrificial love and service.

When you think God may be speaking to you, run it through the "wisdom from above" test. If it doesn't pass, go back to praying and listening. God has more to say.

6. God's voice is confirmed in multiple ways.

In the Old Testament, testimony in court was only considered valid if it was confirmed by two or three witnesses (Deuteronomy 19:15). The principle is repeated in a spiritual context in the New Testament (2 Corinthians 13:1).

Usually, if God tells you something important, He will repeat that message multiple times and in more than one way. He promised Abraham on several occasions that He would one day have descendants even though his wife was barren (Genesis 12:2; 17:1–21; 18:10). He sent numerous prophets to warn Israel to repent as well as to prophesy about the Savior who would one day come.

God knows we need to hear some things more than once. We don't always get it right the first time. We might be confused, unsure if we're hearing correctly or making things up.

If you feel that way sometimes, it's a good thing. It means you are humble enough to recognize you could be wrong. People who are always sure they are hearing God correctly scare me. That's how cults start.

If you think you might be hearing from God, start by checking it against the previous points we've discussed. Does it line up with Scripture? Does it bring peace? Is it quiet but sure? Is it comforting but a little uncomfortable? Does it promote love toward others?

Then, take a look at the following pages. We're going to go through a list of ways God might speak. These "witnesses" will help you determine if that thought, emotion, or dream in your heart comes from God.

WAYS GOD SPEAKS

God is a creative communicator. Maybe the best example of this is when He used a donkey with an attitude to call out a stubborn prophet (see Numbers 22). Mouthy animals are the exception, though. God usually uses more socially acceptable channels of communication. Let's explore some of them.

1. The Bible

As we saw earlier, the Bible is the loudest, clearest, most objective, and most authoritative voice of them all. Most of what we know about God didn't come from a voice whispering to us in the night. It is written in black and white in front of our eyes. All other messages we hear need to be judged against the accurate, unchanging written Word of God.

I'll say it again: God speaks loudest and most consistently through His Word.

If you want to hear God through His Word, though, you have to read it. Don't focus on quantity. It's not a race, and there's no prize in heaven for finishing your Bible reading first.

Read a few verses, then meditate on them. Take your time. Ask God if He wants to speak through them.

If you need help understanding what you read or being consistent in reading, there are lots of study helps available. Bible reading apps, commentaries, and study Bibles can all be invaluable aids. If you think God is saying something, use those aids to see if you can find other verses that talk about the same topic. Talk to someone else if you need another perspective.

The same Holy Spirit who inspired the Word will open it up to you as you read.

2. The Holy Spirit

When you became a follower of Jesus, He sent the Holy Spirit into your heart to take up residence there (Ephesians 1:13). The Holy Spirit is God's presence living in us. He teaches us, guides us, convicts us, encourages us, strengthens us, and helps us.

Often this happens without our being consciously aware that He's even speaking. He brings a verse to mind, or He helps us see a different perspective on something, or He uses our conscience to point out an area we need to correct.

Other times, we are aware it's Him. We "hear" in our spirits a quiet but persistent voice or message that something inside us knows is true. It's hard to describe this in words, but if it's happened to you, then you know what I'm talking about. Pay attention to that voice when you hear it. Seek confirmation in Scripture that what you are hearing is correct. Over time, you will learn to recognize the voice better and better.

Sometimes the Holy Spirit speaks through others in the form of prophecy, which refers to sharing a specific message from God for a person or situation. Prophecy is one of the gifts of the Holy Spirit (1 Corinthians 14:1). When it comes to prophecy, listen with an open heart and a cautious mind. Judge what you hear against Scripture, what you sense in your heart, and what wise counsel says.

Hearing the voice of the Spirit is subjective, as we've already discussed, but it's also very real. Don't stress out about it. Just listen. Develop your spiritual senses to hear His voice. If it's God, He'll make it clear.

3. Wise counsel

God often uses people who have more experience, training, or insight than us to confirm His will and direction. This might include parents, pastors, mentors, therapists, bosses, teachers, counselors, friends, and more.

Wisdom, according to Proverbs, isn't having all the answers, but rather being willing to ask for advice. To listen. To learn. To invite contradictory opinions and multiple points of view. "Plans fail for lack of counsel, but with many advisers they succeed" (Proverbs 15:22).

Other people are no more infallible than you or I, but they do have a valuable point of view. They might confirm what we have already thought. They might point out a blind spot. They might see dangers we don't see. They might have learned something the hard way, and we might as well learn from their pain rather than re-creating it for ourselves.

A word of caution here: Don't let others influence you *too much*. The idea of "counsel" has often been abused, both in the church and outside it.

You don't need someone else to interpret God for you or to stand between you and God. Much damage has been done by people who claim to represent

God and demand submission and obedience from everyone. Please don't blindly follow anyone, even if they claim to speak for God, and even if they seem to have a lot of success, knowledge, or influence.

That is not the kind of counsel I am talking about. Counsel is not about control, but about servanthood. It's not about dominating, but about releasing. It's not about demeaning or condescending, but about empowering. Ignore the narcissists, the control freaks, the abusive "leaders," and anyone who would silence your voice. You don't need them. Look for voices of counsel that serve you, release you, and empower you.

You do need counselors—you just need the right ones. Listen to people who truly love you. People who don't have anything to gain from flattery. People with maturity, wisdom, and humility.

There is no shame in asking for help. Instead, there is safety.

4. Circumstances

God may use circumstances in your life to guide you. He might open a door, or close one permanently, or just close one temporarily until you're ready. Occasionally, He blows one completely off the hinges and shoves you through even though you most definitely do _not_ feel ready.

Proverbs 16:9 says, "In their hearts humans plan their course, but the LORD establishes their steps." Proverbs 20:24 says, "A person's steps are directed by the LORD. How then can anyone understand their own way?" In other words, God is actively involved in guiding our paths.

This doesn't mean we are robots, programmed to do exactly what God has predetermined should happen. But it does mean that God, in His sovereignty and power, is able to direct us even when we don't get it right on our own.

I personally find this to be a huge relief. If I'm trying to make an important decision, I pray about it. I see what the Bible has to say about it. I listen for the Spirit's voice. I get counsel. But sometimes, I still don't have a clear sense of what God is saying.

At that point, if I need to make a decision, I do so. And I trust that God will direct me through circumstances even when I haven't "heard" His voice.

5. Wisdom

God also communicates through our own wisdom. Technically, this might not always be God "speaking." But He created our brains in the first place, He invented common sense and logic, and He gives us divine wisdom, so I think it's appropriate in this list.

We looked at James 1:5 earlier: "If any of you lacks wisdom, you should ask God, who gives generously to all without finding fault, and it will be given to you." Solomon's only request was God's wisdom, and that request delighted the heart of God (1 Kings 3). God clearly values wisdom and uses it to guide us.

Wisdom is more than just knowledge. Knowledge is information, but wisdom is the ability to know what to do with that information. Through our natural abilities, experience, study, and humble willingness to learn, we gain wisdom for healthy decision-making.

The Bible has an entire book—Proverbs—dedicated to wisdom. If you want to grow in wisdom, there is no better place to start than meditating on the insights in those chapters. James is another great book.

Don't underestimate your own mind. Your own ideas. Your own perspective. No, you don't have all the answers; and yes, you should pray, research options, and get counsel.

But you bring a lot to the table too. You will often have the best perspective (next to God) on what you should do. Lean in to wisdom, and it will guide you.

6. Dreams, visions, signs, and angels

It might seem odd in our hyper-rationalistic Western culture to even talk about God speaking to us in dreams or visions, through signs, or with a visit from an actual angel. In my experience, at least, these means of communication are rarer today than the ones above. But in the Bible, these were common ways He spoke. God can and does use dreams, visions, signs, and even visits from angels to communicate with people today.

Because these are so subjective, if you do have a dream or other experience that you believe comes from God, I'd encourage you not only to compare what you hear with Scripture, but also to talk it over with a trusted mentor or friend who can help you evaluate it. Don't blindly accept something as being from God, but don't be too quick to reject it either.

I often remember what Mary, the mother of Jesus, did when she saw unbelievable things happening in her life. "But Mary treasured up all these things and pondered them in her heart" (Luke 2:19; see also verse 51). If there is something you don't understand, just wait. Ponder it. Store it in your heart until God makes it clear.

7. Creation

Have you ever asked yourself where the idea of beauty came from? Not the recognition that something is beautiful, but the concept itself. It came from God. He is beautiful, and He gave us the ability to appreciate and love beauty. He paints daily masterpieces in the sky every morning and every night, and we get to enjoy them.

Psalm 19:1 says, "The heavens declare the glory of God; the skies proclaim the work of his hands." Romans 1:20 says, "For since the creation of the world God's invisible qualities—his eternal power and divine nature—have been clearly seen, being understood from what has been made, so that people are without excuse."

Nature has a voice. It testifies to God's existence, power, and faithfulness. It reminds us that no matter what is happening in our crazy day-to-day world, the universe remains. God remains. He is greater than all the things that are worrying us. No matter what, He won't change, and He won't forsake us.

If you need to hear from God, try getting closer to His creation. Go camping in the mountains. Take a day trip to the beach. Go for a hike. Do it alone, or with someone who has the gift of shutting up when it's appropriate.

225

Find a place with a good view, and just sit. Contemplate. Be still.

God created everything you see: from the vast expanse of the sky above to the intricacies of the plants at your feet.

You're in safe hands.

NOW WHAT?

When you do hear from God, respond.

Listening is not passive, but active. We hear and obey. We listen and respond.

If He tells you He loves you and you are precious to Him, believe it. If He nudges you to make a change in some area, ask for His help and then do it. If He challenges you to take a risk, obey in faith.

You can't expect God to continue speaking to you if you're ignoring the things He's already said.

You can't expect God to continue speaking to you if you're ignoring the things He's already said. Healthy relationships don't work that way. You won't always get it right—the listening or the obeying. None of us does.

But if your heart is to hear and obey God, He will honor that.

That's the essence of prayer, after all: our hearts drawing closer to God's heart.

Hearing from God is a learning process. It's a life-long journey. And it's a wonderful one, full of surprises and treasures and hidden delight. Get to know God.

Listen.

He is speaking.

Start and end with prayer

In this hectic, random, noisy life, peace is not an impossible dream.

It's a promise. It's a gift from God, one we both long for and desperately need.

I'm not talking about the peace that comes from having everything figured out and under control, but the peace that descends from heaven itself. The peace of God that passes understanding. The peace we experience when we cast our cares upon the one who cares for us.

It's a peace that starts and ends with prayer. Are you worried about everything because you pray about nothing? It's time to flip the script.

Be worried for *nothing* because you pray about *everything*.

That's the lifestyle of peace and joy that God is calling you into through prayer. It's your future as a child of God.

Jesus says, "Here I am! I stand at the door and knock. If anyone hears my voice and opens the door, I will come in and eat with that person, and they with me" (Revelation 3:20).

Sometimes people use that verse to describe salvation, but the words were actually written to believers. Jesus wants to be with us. Not as a judge putting us on trial, or a boss doing an employee review, or an emperor berating a servant.

As a _friend_.

Jesus wants to stroll through the door of our hearts, sit down next to us with the drink of His choice, and just hang out. He wants to hear what's on our hearts and minds. He wants us to express what is worrying us or inspiring us or challenging us. And He wants to share with us the peace, perspective, and power of God.

I know we've just spent a couple hundred pages doing a deep dive into the intricacies of prayer, but the bottom line is that prayer is not hard. It's natural. It flows unforced from authentic relationship.

You can't really "do it wrong," and you can't be "bad at it." Yes, you can get better, but nobody is grading your progress or judging the eloquence of your prayers. Least of all God. He's just happy to hear from you, to be honest. And excited about partnering with you for the future.

So, just pray!

However you want.

Wherever you're at.

Whenever you feel like it.

For whatever you need.

It really is that simple.

Acknowledgments

To my wife, Julia. The queen of our world. The boss. Where would I be without you? Answer: lost; without salvation, food, clothing, and laughter.

You are truly the greatest.

To our children. I adore each of you. Thank you for making our home a place of constant fun, chaos, and love.

To Zoe church. Thank you to our amazing community. The greatest people on the planet. I love you all so very much!

To my parents. Thank you for your love and faithfulness. You guys are the gold standard.

To our board. Your covering and leadership continue to shine bright each year. Thank you for your friendship and constant support.

To Justin Jaquith, author of authors. I love the way you think and write. Love talking things out and processing truth with you. Let's just keep doing this thing together. Perhaps God is calling us to write in Cabo next time (just thinking out loud here).

To Whitney Gossett. We started from the bottom, now we're here (wherever *here* is LOL). . . . Thanks for believing in us, taking a risk on us, and always thinking about new, creative things for us to do! You're the greatest!

To Roman and Erika Bozhko. No one would ever see or hear about this book without you guys. Thanks for being our friends . . . and the creative geniuses that you are. We love you both.

Pray About Everything

Don't worry about anything;
instead, pray about everything.
Tell God what you need,
and thank him for all he has done.
PHILIPPIANS 4:6

Remember This When You Pray

》 *ANYONE CAN PRAY*

"If my people who are called by My name will humble themselves, and pray and seek My face, and turn from their wicked ways, then I will hear from heaven, and will forgive their sin and heal their land." **2 CHRONICLES 7:14**

"Let us therefore come boldly to the throne of grace, that we may obtain mercy and find grace to help in time of need." **HEBREWS 4:16**

》 *PRAYER IS SIMPLY TALKING TO GOD*

"Now this is the confidence that we have in Him, that if we ask anything according to His will, He hears us." **1 JOHN 5:14**

》 *JESUS TAUGHT US TO PRAY*

"This, then, is how you should pray: 'Our Father in heaven, hallowed be your name.'" **MATTHEW 6:9–13**

》 *PRAY ALL THE TIME, ANYWHERE, ABOUT ANYTHING*

"Don't worry about anything; instead, pray about everything. Tell God what you need, and thank him for all he has done. Then you will experience God's peace, which exceeds anything we can understand. His peace will guard your hearts and minds as you live in Christ Jesus." **PHILIPPIANS 4:6–7**

In Your Daily Prayers, Use These Four Points To Help Create Genuine, Authentic, And Effective Prayers:

1. PRAY SPECIFICALLY **1 JOHN 5:15**
2. PRAY PASSIONATELY **JAMES 5:16**
3. PRAY CONFIDENTLY **PSALM 24:3–4**
4. PRAY GOD'S WORD **ROMANS 10:17**

A.C.T.S.
PRAYER MODEL

A—ADORATION
C—CONFESSION
T—THANKSGIVING
S—SUPPLICATION

1 FAITH

- Without faith it is impossible to please God. I will come to Him believing that He rewards those who sincerely seek Him. **HEBREWS 11:6**
- Lord, I believe, but help my unbelief. **MARK 9:24**
- I will not be afraid, for I know that Jesus will calm the storm. **MATTHEW 8:26**
- I will be strengthened in faith, giving glory to God. **ROMANS 4:20**
- I walk by faith, not by sight. **2 CORINTHIANS 5:7**
- I will fight the good fight, finish my race, and keep the faith. **2 TIMOTHY 4:7**

2 PROVISION

- And God is able to make all grace abound toward me, that I, always having all sufficiency in all things, may have an abundance for every good work. **2 CORINTHIANS 9:8**
- Consider the ravens, for they neither sow nor reap, which have neither storehouse nor barn; and God feeds them. Of how much more value am I than the birds? **LUKE 12:24**
- I will seek the kingdom of God first and His righteousness, and all these things will be added to me. **MATTHEW 6:33**
- My God will supply all of my needs according to His riches in glory by Christ Jesus. **PHILIPPIANS 4:19**
- The Lord is my shepherd; I shall not want. **PSALM 23:1**
- I was young and now I am old, yet I have never seen the righteous forsaken or their children begging bread. **PSALM 37:25**
- He who did not spare His own Son, but delivered Him up for us all, how shall He not with Him also freely give us all things? **ROMANS 8:32**

3 RELATIONSHIPS

- I will have fervent love for one another above all things, for love will cover a multitude of sins. **1 PETER 4:8**
- I will encourage others and build other people up. **1 THESSALONIANS 5:11**
- I will not let any unwholesome talk come out of my mouth, but only what is helpful for building others up according to their needs, that it may benefit those who listen. **EPHESIANS 4:29**
- I will be completely humble and gentle; patient, bearing with one another in love. Making every effort to keep the unity of the Spirit through the bond of peace. **EPHESIANS 4:2–3**
- A friend loves at all times, and a brother is born for a time of adversity. **PROVERBS 17:17**

4 HEALING

- Heal me, O Lord, and I will be healed; save me and I will be saved, for You are the one I praise. **JEREMIAH 17:14**
- Is anyone among you sick? Let them call the elders of the church to pray over them and anoint them with oil in the name of the Lord. And the prayer offered in faith will make the sick person well; the Lord will raise them up. If they have sinned, they will be forgiven. **JAMES 5:14–15**
- I will not fear, because God is with me. I will not be discouraged, because God will strengthen me and help me. **ISAIAH 41:10**

- Jesus was pierced for my transgressions, He was crushed for our iniquities; the punishment that brought us peace was on Him, and by His wounds I am healed. **ISAIAH 53:4–5**
- But I will restore you to health and heal your wounds, declares the LORD. **JEREMIAH 30:17**
- Praise the Lord, my soul, and forget not all His benefits - who forgives all my sins and heals my diseases, who redeems my life from the pit and crowns me with love and compassion. **PSALM 103:2–4**

5 STRESS & ANXIETY

- My flesh and my heart may fail, but God is the strength of my heart and my portion forever. **PSALM 73:26**
- For God has not given me a spirit of fear, but of power and of love and of a sound mind. **2 TIMOTHY 1:7**
- When anxiety is great within me, your consolation brings me joy. **PSALM 94:19**
- I will not be anxious about anything, but in every situation, by prayer and petition, with thanksgiving, I will present my requests to God. **PHILIPPIANS 4:6**
- I will cast all my anxiety on Him because He cares for me. **1 PETER 5:7**

6 WISDOM

- The Lord gives wisdom; from His mouth come knowledge and understanding. **PROVERBS 2:6**
- I will not forsake wisdom, and she will protect me; I will love wisdom, and she will watch over me. The beginning of wisdom is this: get wisdom. Though it costs all I have, I will get understanding. **PROVERBS 4:6–7**
- But the wisdom that comes from heaven is first of all pure; then peace-loving, considerate, submissive, full of mercy and good fruit, impartial and sincere. **JAMES 3:17**
- My heart plans my way, but the Lord directs my steps. **PROVERBS 16:9**

7 JOY

- I will count it all joy when I fall into various trials, knowing that the testing of my faith produces patience. **JAMES 1:2**
- Hear, Lord, and be merciful to me; Lord, be my help. You turned my wailing into dancing; you removed my sackcloth and clothed me with joy. **PSALM 30:10–11**
- The joy of the Lord is my strength. **NEHEMIAH 8:10**
- May the God of hope fill me with all joy and peace in believing, so that by the power of the Holy Spirit I may abound in hope. **ROMANS 15:13**

8 PURITY

- To the pure, all things are pure. **TITUS 1:15**
- Blessed are the pure in heart, for they will see God. **MATTHEW 5:8**
- Create in me a pure heart, O God, and renew a steadfast spirit within me. **PSALM 51:10**
- How can a young person stay on the path of purity? By living according to Your word. **PSALM 119:9**
- Whatever is true, whatever is noble, whatever is right, whatever is pure, whatever is lovely, whatever is admirable—if anything is excellent or praiseworthy—I will think about such things. **PHILIPPIANS 4:8**

9 VICTORY

- If God is for me, who can be against me? **ROMANS 8:31**
- But thanks be to God! He gives me the victory through our Lord Jesus Christ. **1 CORINTHIANS 15:57**
- Finally, be strong in the Lord and in His mighty power. **EPHESIANS 6:10**
- Whoever is born of God overcomes the world. And this is the victory that has overcome the world—our faith. **1 JOHN 5:4**

10 PEACE

- I will let the peace of God rule my heart. **COLOSSIANS 3:15**
- Peace I leave with you; my peace I give you. I do not give to you as the world gives. Do not let your hearts be troubled and do not be afraid. **JOHN 14:27**
- The Lord of peace Himself gives me peace at all times and in every way. **2 THESSALONIANS 3:16**
- And the peace of God, which transcends all understanding, will guard my heart and my mind in Christ Jesus. **PHILIPPIANS 4:7**

Learn more about prayer and fasting
at zoechurch.org/pray

Notes

Chapter 2 Relaxing on a roller coaster

1. American Psychological Association, *Stress in America 2020: A National Mental Health Crisis*, www.apa.org/news/press/releases/stress/2020/sia-mental-health-crisis.pdf, 1.

Chapter 3 Pour your own cereal

1. Christina Desmarais, "Science Says the Most Successful Kids Have Parents Who Do These 9 Things," *Inc.com*, September 9, 2017, https://www.inc.com/kimberly-weisul/shearshare-tye -caldwell-studying-relationships-kindergarten-paying-off.html.

Chapter 4 God is not your dentist

1. Albert Bandura, "Self-Efficacy Mechanism in Human Agency," *American Psychologist* 37, no. 2 (February 1982): 123, https://pdfs.semanticscholar.org/8bee/c556fe7a650120544a99e9e063e- b8fcd987b.pdf.

Chapter 5 I'd rather be at the beach

1. e.e. Cummings, *Complete Poems: 1904–1962* , ed. George J. Firmage (United Kingdom: Liver- right Publishing Corporation, 2016), n.p.

2. Attributed. Rolf Edberg. www.goodreads.com/quotes/264872-in-still-moments-by-the -sea-life-seems-large-drawn-and.

3. The Notorious B.I.G. "Juicy (It Was All a Dream)," *Ready to Die* (Bad Boy, Arista, 1994).

Chapter 6 The problem with birthdays

1. John Mark Comer, *The Ruthless Elimination of Hurry: How to Stay Emotionally Healthy and Spiritually Alive in the Chaos of the Modern World* (Colorado Springs: Waterbrook, 2019), 54–55.

Chapter 7 Have you tried resetting it?

1. Peter Scazzero, *Emotionally Healthy Spirituality* (Grand Rapids, MI: Zondervan, 2017), 7.

Chapter 8 Growing pains

1. Gerhard Kittel, Gerhard Friedrich, & Geoffrey W. Bromiley, eds., *Theological Dictionary of the New Testament* (Grand Rapids, MI: W.B. Eerdmans, 1985), 1164.

2. Jillian Michaels, Mariska van Aalst, and Christine Darwin, *Master Your Metabolism: The 3 Diet Secrets to Naturally Balancing Your Hormones for a Hot and Healthy Body!* (Harmony/Rodale, 2009), 21.

Chapter 10 How to dodge ducks

1. James Clear, *Atomic Habits* (New York: Avery, 2018), 28.

Chapter 11 These prayers are a waste of time

1. Kittel, Friedrich, and Bromiley, *Theological Dictionary of the New Testament*, 1236.

2. Mary Oliver, *Thirst* (Boston: Beacon Press, 2006), 37.

3. A. T. Robertson, *Word Pictures in the New Testament*, Mat. 6:7 (Nashville, TN: Broadman Press, 1933).

4. Katherine Schwarzenegger, *The Gift of Forgiveness* (New York: Penguin, 2020), 7.

5. Fred R. Shapiro, "Who Wrote the Serenity Prayer?" *The Chronicle of Higher Education*, April 28, 2014, www.chronicle.com/article/who-wrote-the-serenity-prayer.

Chapter 12 The cycle of prayer

1. Luke Dormehl, "The oddly uplifting story of the Apple co-founder who sold his stake for $800," *Cult of Mac*, December 3, 2014, www.cultofmac.com/304686/ron-wayne-apple-co-founder.

Chapter 13 Spiritual bypassing is not spiritual at all

1. Philip B. Clark, Amanda L. Giordano, Craig S. Cashwell, and Todd F. Lewis, "The Straight Path to Healing: Using Motivational Interviewing to Address Spiritual Bypass," *Journal of Counseling & Development* 91, no. 1, (January 2013), 87.

2. Clark, Giordano, Cashwell, and Lewis, "The Straight Path to Healing," 88.

Chapter 14 The dark side of prayer

1. Michael Greshko, "China just landed on the far side of the moon: What comes next?" *National Geographic*, January 2, 2019, www.nationalgeographic.com/science/article/china-change-4-historic-landing-moon-far-side-explained.

2. Ernest Kurtz and Katherine Ketcham, *The Spirituality of Imperfection* (New York: Bantam Books, 1992), 61.

Chapter 15 Lord, teach us to bowl

1. "What is Forgiveness?" *Greater Good Magazine*. https://greatergood.berkeley.edu/topic/forgiveness/definition.

2. Craig S. Keener, *The IVP Bible Background Commentary: New Testament*, Second Edition (Downer's Grove, IL: Intervarsity, 2014), "Matthew."

3. Lisa Rogak, ed., _Impatient Optimist: Bill Gates in His Own Words_ (London: Hardie Grant Books, 2012), 118.

Chapter 16 These are dangerous prayers

1. C. S. Lewis, _The Lion, the Witch and the Wardrobe_ (New York: Scholastic, 1995), 79–80.

2. "NBA Advanced Stats," NBA (2021), www.nba.com/stats.

3. "Kobe Bryant as missed the most career field goals, with 14,481 misses," www.statmuse.com /nba/ask/who-has-the-most-missed-field-goals-in-nba-history.

4. Chris Ballard, "Kobe Bryant on growing old, players he respects and finding his inner Zen," _Sports Illustrated_, August 26, 2014, https://www.si.com/nba/2014/08/26/kobe-bryant-lakers -dwight-howard-tony-allen-retirement.

5. Donald B. Kraybill, _The Upside-Down Kingdom_ (Harrisonburg: Herald, 2011), 15–16.

Chapter 17 What's on the menu?

1. Melissa Gouty, "4 Reasons Why Reading Out Loud Is Actually Good for You," LiteratureLust .com, November 10, 2020, www.literaturelust.com/post/4-reasons-why-reading-out-loud-is -actually-good-for-you. Lottie Miles, "5 Surprising Benefits of Thinking Aloud, Backed by Science," The Learning Mind, December 31, 2019, www.learning-mind.com/thinking-aloud -benefits.

2. "Cathedral Building in the Middle Ages," Durham World Heritage Site, accessed September 7, 2021, www.durhamworldheritagesite.com/learn/architecture/cathedral/construction.

3. "Worship: Information Sheet: Lectio Divina," accessed September 7, 2021, www.anglican communion.org/media/253799/1-What-is-Lectio-Divina.pdf.

About the Author

Chad Veach is the founder and lead pastor of Zoe Church, a dynamic community in the heart of Los Angeles, California. For the past 20 years, he has dedicated his life to ministry and preaching the gospel. In addition to leading Zoe, he is an international speaker; the author of three books: *Help! I Work With People*, *Faith Forward Future*, and *Unreasonable Hope*; and the host of Leadership Lean In, a top charting leadership podcast. Chad and his wife, Julia, reside in Los Angeles with their four children: Georgia, Winston, Maverick, and Clive.

More from Chad Veach

Becoming a great leader is more about prioritizing self-awareness and people skills than innovative ideas and high levels of productivity. With his transparent and relatable storytelling, Chad Veach addresses three phases of becoming a quality leader, and urges you to lean in to your leadership potential regardless of your level of influence or experience.

Help! I Work with People

BETHANYHOUSE

 Stay up to date on your favorite books and authors with our free e-newsletters. Sign up today at bethanyhouse.com.

 facebook.com/BHPnonfiction

 @bethany_house

 @bethany_house_nonfiction